GYMNASTIC ACT~~IVITY~~

PE LESSON PLANS

year 3 COMPLETE TEACHING PROGRAMME

WITH

LEAPFROGS

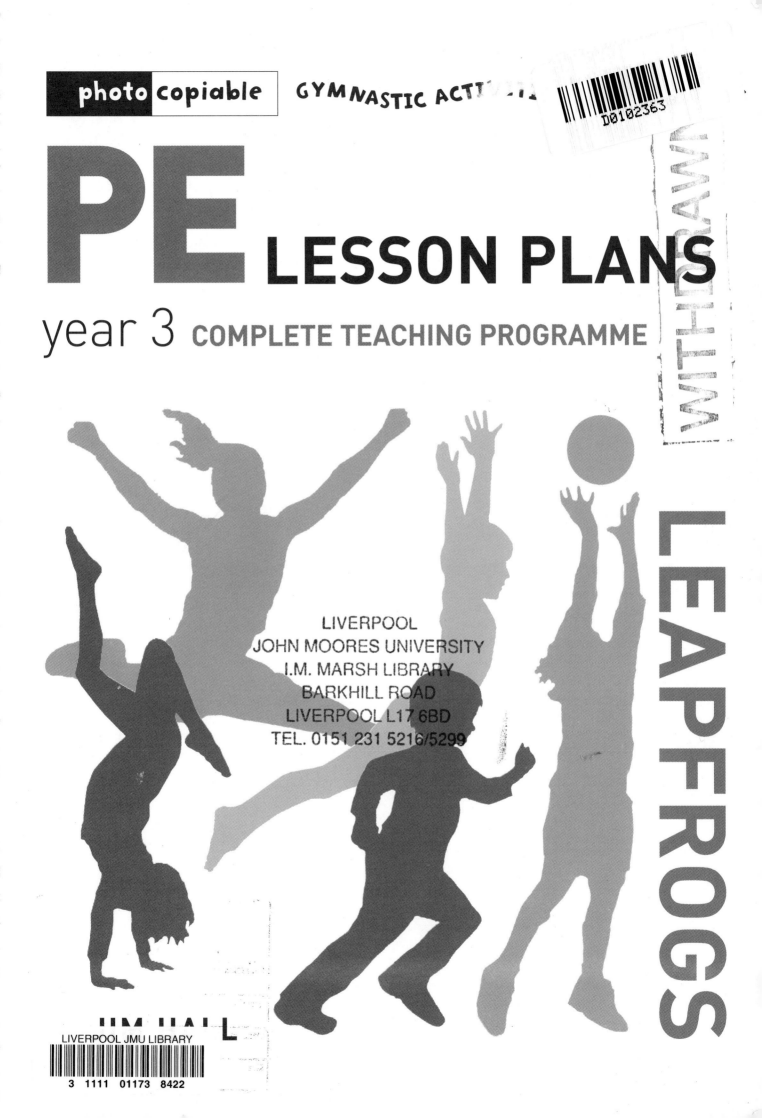

JM HALL

Published in 2005 by A & C Black Publishers Ltd
37 Soho Square, London W1D 3QZ
www.acblack.com

ISBN 0 7136 7214 5

A CIP record for this book is available from the British Library.

Note: While every effort has been made to ensure that the content of this book is as technically accurate and as sound as possible, neither the author nor the publisher can accept responsibility for any injury or loss sustained as a result of the use of this material.

A & C Black uses paper produced with elemental chlorine-free pulp, harvested from managed sustainable forests.

Acknowledgements
Cover and inside design by Peter Bailey
Illustrations by Eleanor King

Typeset in 10pt DIN Regular.

Printed and bound in Great Britain by Martins the Printers, Berwick upon Tweed.

Contents

Introduction

The near total disappearance of out-of-school play, caused by traffic increase, increased watching of television, participation in video games, and parental concern when children are out of sight, means that regular and vigorous Physical Education lessons, where girls and boys move, share and play together, are more important than ever if our children are to achieve their optimum physical, social, emotional and intellectual development. Physical Education is central to the area of physical development within the school curriculum and makes a unique contribution to an all-round education by providing opportunities for every child to experience movement activities at first hand. They do not read, hear or talk about them. They do, feel, experience, practise, develop and learn the activities and skills.

The infant and junior school years deserve to be called 'The great age of physical development and Physical Education', with children displaying an insatiable appetite for movement and the learning of every kind of physical skill. Primary school Physical Education lessons are doubly rewarding. They satisfy, on the one hand, the natural biological need for movement in growing, naturally active children, providing pleasure, satisfaction, an outlet for restless surplus energy and a sense of well-being, which enhances the quality of school life and childhood. On the other hand, the wide range of skills learned and enjoyed will be remembered by the body for a great many years, giving continued enjoyment and, potentially, a life-long involvement in enjoyable, sociable and healthy physical activities.

The following pages aim to help class teachers and schools with their thinking about, planning, teaching and developing their Physical Education lessons and programme.

Jim Hall
March 2005

Gymnastic Activities

Introduction to Gymnastic Activities

Gymnastic Activities is an indoor lesson that includes varied floorwork on a clear floor, unimpeded by apparatus, followed by varied apparatus work, which should take up just over half of the lesson time. Ideally, the apparatus will have been positioned around the sides and ends of the room adjacent to where it will be used. This allows each of the five or six groups of pupils to lift, carry and place their apparatus in a very short time because no set will need to be moved more than 3–5 metres. The lesson is traditionally of 30 minutes duration.

Unlike the teaching of Geography and History, for example, where the teacher has a variety of resources to turn to as well as new places and centuries, the teacher of Gymnastic Activities meets the same floor and apparatus week after week, with the continual problem of making the lessons newly interesting, challenging, exciting and different every month. The teacher is central to the success and enjoyment of the lessons because he or she is the source of the stimuli that make the lessons physical, educational, vigorous and enjoyable.

The following pages aim, first of all, to provide a focus for a staffroom togetherness and a unity of purpose, attitude and sense of direction among all the staff concerned. Without this sense of unity, the diversity of approaches, attitudes and standards can mean that there is no continuity of expectations or programme, and a less than satisfactory level of achievement.

Second, the following pages provide a full scheme of work for Year 3 Gymnastic Activities. There is a lesson plan and accompanying page of detailed explanatory notes for every month, designed to help teachers and schools with ideas for lessons that are progressive and implement NC requirements. The 'NC elements being emphasised' headings provide the practical help that is completely missing from the revised 1999 National Curriculum Physical Education document's two sentences about what 'Pupils should be taught' and about what 'Pupils should be able to demonstrate.'

Why we teach Gymnastic Activities

Ideally, the expressions of intent below known as 'Aims' represent the combined views of all the staff concerned.

Aim 1

Inspire vigorous physical activity to promote normal healthy growth, suppleness and strength. 'Remember that you are, first and foremost, purveyors of action. Let your lessons be scenes of busy activity.' Physical Education is most valuable when the pupils' participation is enthusiastic, vigorous and whole-hearted. All subsequent aims for a good programme depend on achieving this first aim.

Aim 2

Teach physical skills to develop neat, skilful, well-controlled, versatile movement. We want pupils to enjoy moving well, safely and confidently in a variety of situations. Physical Education makes a unique contribution to a child's physical development because the activities are experienced at first hand, as they do, feel, practise, and learn the activities and skills.

Aim 3

Help pupils to become good learners as well as good movers. Knowledge, understanding and learning are achieved through a combination of doing, feeling, and experiencing physical activity. Pupils are challenged to think for themselves, making decisions about their actions.

Aim 4

Develop pupils' self-confidence and self-esteem by appreciating the importance of achievement, physically, to young pupils; by helping them to achieve; and by recognising and sharing such achievement with others. 'An individual's regard for and attitude to his or her physical self, especially at primary school age, is important to the development of self-image and to the value given to self.'

Aim 5

Develop desirable social qualities, helping pupils get on well with one another by bringing them together in mutual endeavours. Friendly, co-operative, close relationships are an ever-present feature of Physical Education lessons.

Aim 6

Through Gymnastic Activities, and Dance and Games, we try to satisfy every pupil's entitlement to achieve physical competence in a broad and balanced Physical Education programme. We want the Physical Education programme to make its unique contribution to an all-round education, and to make a special contribution to encouraging participation in a healthy lifestyle, long after pupils have left school.

Teaching Gymnastic Activities

The teacher, without assistance from classroom teaching aids, is the central inspiration of the lesson. An enthusiastic, well-prepared teacher can inspire whole-hearted, vigorous and thoughtful responses, which can lead to success, achievement and feelings of well-being and enhanced self-esteem.

The lesson plan is the teacher's essential guide and reminder. Only by referring to the plan can the busy teacher remind him or herself of the lesson's total content. July's end-of-year lesson will only be at a more advanced stage than the previous September's lesson if all the lessons in between have been recorded and progressed.

Each lesson usually runs for four to five weeks to allow children to practise, repeat, learn, remember and develop the skills involved.

Try to avoid 'dead spots' and queues. 'Be found working, not waiting' should be understood by all. Those moments when the class is standing, sitting, queuing, or doing nothing must be kept to a minimum.

'Direct' teaching, where the teacher decides what the class will do, is used to: gain quick responses, good attention, and class control; teach the class the safe way to lift, carry, place and use apparatus; teach the safe, correct way to perform many of the skills; provide the stimulus of a direct request which most children find enjoyable, and to help the less 'inventive'; concentrate on and improve poor work by making all pupils aware of the main feature in an activity.

'Shared choice' or 'indirect' teaching is the most common type of teaching used, and happens when the children work at activities of their choice within limits set by the teacher. With the inexperienced, the limitations are very slight. 'Show me how you can travel along the bench' leaves much freedom of choice. As pupils progress, more challenging limits are placed: 'As you travel along the bench, can you include a beautifully stretched balance and a change of direction?' Shared choice teaching results in a wide variety of responses. When accompanied by class observation and pupil and teacher comment, it rapidly increases the class repertoire.

Demonstration, observation and comment by the children and the teacher are an essential teaching technique. We remember what we see, and pupils should be directed to see examples of good-quality work, variety and the safe, correct way to do things. They can also be shown the exact meaning of the words and gymnastic terminology being used. All can watch one, two or a small group. Half of the class can watch the other half. Each can watch a partner. It should be understood by the observers that they will be asked to comment after the demonstration so that observation becomes a learning activity that aims to assist everyone. 'Watch Susan and Gary as they do their sequences. Tell me how their work differs, and look out for changes of speed or direction that you like as interesting contrasts.' Further class practice should always follow a demonstration so that everyone can try to include some of the good features praised and commented on.

A pattern for teaching and improving a Gymnastic Activities action

'Travelling' is the example used.

1. Move quickly into action. With few words, clearly explain the task and challenge the class to start. For example, 'Can you plan to travel, using your feet, sometimes going forwards, and sometimes in another direction?

2. While the class is working, emphasise the main points, one at a time. There is no need to stop a well-behaved class that is working quietly every time you want to make a teaching point. 'Find quiet spaces in all parts of the room – the sides, ends, corners as well as the middle.' 'Travel on straight lines, never curving around, following someone.' 'Look over your shoulder if going backwards.'

3. Identify and praise good work while the class is working. The teacher needs to circulate around the outside of the room, looking in to see as much of the work as possible. 'Well done, Steve. I liked your skipping forwards and bouncing sideways.' 'Joanne, your hopscotch is a great idea.' 'Sarah, your slow, careful running backwards, with high knees lifting, is a neat, safe way to travel.'

4. Demonstrations accompanied by teacher comment are the quickest way to increase the class repertoire. It saves time if the demonstrators have been told which aspect of movement they are about to be asked to demonstrate. 'We will be looking at your beautifully stretched body in your jumps, and the soft, quiet way you let your knees and ankles give when you land.' Or 'Stop and watch Richard's lively, quiet bouncing with feet parting and closing, going sideways. And look at Clara's galloping backwards with a strong arm swing.' Beware of stopping the class too often to use a demonstration. Make these stoppages brief, between 12 and 15 seconds.

5 Further practice should always follow a demonstration with reminders of the good things seen. Pupils enjoy copying something they never thought of trying, particularly when it has been warmly praised and approved of. 'Thank you for those excellent demonstrations. Practise again, everyone, and try to improve your travelling by using something of what you have just seen. Use your whole body strongly, but quietly. Your feet can travel together or apart, or one after the other.'

6 Demonstrations (by an individual, a small group or half the class) with follow-up comments by the pupils are used to let pupils reflect on and evaluate their own and others' performances. Such comments and judgements guide the next stage of planning for improvement. 'Watch this group of four working and tell me which travelling actions you like best, and say which directions you saw being used.' This is followed by a brief look at the pupils mentioned.

7 Demonstrators and those making comments are thanked and more class practice lets everyone try some of the good things seen. Beware of using demonstrations with follow-up comments more than once or twice in the lesson because they are time-consuming.

Apparatus work

System A The apparatus is never brought out because the teacher feels insecure and incapable of organising it, and fearful for the safety of the children. The extended floorwork sessions that are substituted for the proper lessons frustrate the children who remember the excitement of apparatus work from previous years, and they behave badly, making the teacher even more unwilling to risk bringing out the apparatus.

System B At the beginning of the morning or afternoon, before lessons start, the apparatus is brought out and then left in position for every class. This system, usually put in place by 'apparatus monitors' pupils, the school caretaker or welfare staff, whose apparatus layout applies to all classes:

a gives no credit to the intelligence and ability of children, who enjoy and are perfectly capable of handling apparatus

b is a source of frustration to those teachers (often new arrivals) who know that it is unsatisfactory

c prevents the safe teaching of floorwork

d stifles the development of any standards

e breaches the NC requirement that 'Pupils should be taught how to lift, carry, place and use equipment safely.'

System C All classes do floorwork and apparatus work, with the apparatus being moved from a storeroom outside the hall, or from the end of the hall, assembled, used and then returned to the remote storeroom or end of hall, every lesson. This time-consuming system, with pile-ups at doors or one end of the hall, can take up to 5 minutes of the lesson time, before and after apparatus work, instead of the minute, or less, needed in the next and recommended system.

System D This requires the approval and co-operation of every member of staff who teaches Gymnastic Activities, and is a system that will have been initiated by the Head, the subject co-ordinator, or by a combined staff decision.

Before lessons start in the mornings or afternoons, the portable apparatus will be placed at the sides and ends of the hall, adjacent to where it will be used. By only having to lift and carry a short distance, very little time is lost by the five or six groups of five or six pupils.

From their regular starting positions, groups rotate clockwise, probably with time to work at three different sets. At the end of the apparatus work the children return to their starting places to put away the apparatus they originally brought out. Once again, little time is needed because the children are experienced in moving their own apparatus and know exactly where it has to be placed, around the sides and ends of the hall. The floor is now clear for the incoming class.

In the next lesson the groups will move anti-clockwise to work at the other three sets of apparatus.

Fixed and portable apparatus

In the lesson plans that follow, the equipment continually being referred to and shown in the apparatus layouts includes the following items:

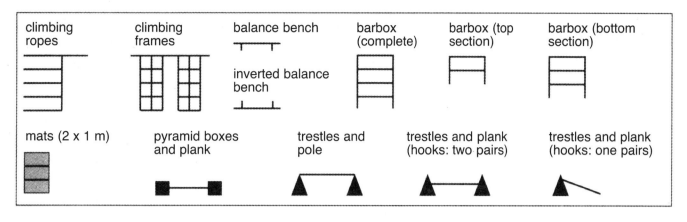

Minimum number recommended:

- ○ 12 × mats (2 × 1 m)
- ○ 3 × balance benches
- ○ 1 × barbox that can be divided into two smaller boxes by lifting off the top section; the remaining lower section should have a platform fitted
- ○ 1 × pair pyramid boxes and one plank
- ○ 1 × pair of 3 ft (0.9 m), 3 ft 6 in (1 m), and 4 ft 6 in (1.4 m) trestles
- ○ 1 metal pole to join pairs of trestles
- ○ 2 planks with two pairs of hooks
- ○ 2 planks with one pair of hooks

Safe practice and accident prevention

1 Good supervision by the teacher at all times is the main contributor to safety in Physical Education lessons. Being there with the class and being in positions from which to see the majority of the pupils is essential. In his or her circulation of the room, teaching and observing, the teacher generally will be on the outside looking inwards, to ensure that as few performers as possible are out of sight behind his or her back.

2 Good behaviour, with its well-ordered, quiet, safe environment, must be continually insisted on until it becomes an automatic part of the lesson. There is nothing for pupils to talk about, apart from on those occasions when the teacher asks for comments on a demonstration or how they think they are responding.

A clearly stated challenge or task which asks for a thoughtful, planned response precludes all chattering. Talking usually means that the class has not been given something to attend to or work towards.

The ultimate aim is a 'doubly quiet' class whose beautifully controlled and quiet movements are matched by a complete absence of inessential talking.

3 Sensible, safe clothing means that there will be no watches, jewellery, rings, long trousers that catch heels, long sleeves that catch fingers, unbunched hair that impedes vision, or socks without shoes.

Barefoot work is recommended because it is quiet, provides a safe, strong grip on apparatus being climbed or jumped from, and enhances the appearance of the performances, particularly when the body is inverted. The small muscles of the foot and ankles are able to work and develop as they grip, stretch, balance, support, push and receive the body weight.

4 Good teaching that develops skilled movement, confidence and self-control goes a long way to producing safe movement.

5 A planned, written-down lesson appropriate to the age of the class means that the children are always working at something specific rather than 'doing anything we like', which could include foolhardy jumping from a high bar.

6 The development in every child of a sense of responsibility and a caring attitude towards self and others is essential and expresses itself in careful, controlled movements and a sensible sharing of floor and apparatus space.

7 The hall should be at a good working temperature with windows and doors being opened or closed as necessary. All potentially dangerous chairs, tables, trolleys or pianos should be pushed against a wall or into a corner. Sockets for receiving securing pins of ropes and climbing frames should be regularly cleared of the cleaning substances which harden and block the sockets.

National Curriculum requirements for Gymnastics Activities –
Key Stage 2: The Main Features

'The government believes that two hours of physical activity a week, including the National Curriculum for Physical Education and extra-curricular activities, should be an aspiration for all schools. This applies to all stages.'

Programme of study   *Pupils should be taught to:*

a   create and perform fluent sequences on the floor and using apparatus
b   include variations in level, speed and directions in their sequences.

Attainment target   *Pupils should be able to demonstrate that they can:*

a   link skill, techniques and ideas and apply them appropriately, showing precision, control and fluency
b   compare and comment on skills, techniques and ideas used in own and others' work and use this understanding to improve their own performances by modifying and refining skills and techniques.

Main NC headings when considering assessment of progression and expectation

○ **Planning** – in a focused, thoughtful, safe way, thinking ahead to an intended outcome. The set criteria are used and there is evidence of originality and variety.

○ **Performing and improving performance** – pupils work hard, concentrating on the main feature of the task, to present a neat, efficient, poised and confident performance, totally under control. They practise to improve, making actions clearer and more accurate, and to be able to remember and repeat them.

○ **Linking actions** – pupils build longer, more complex sequences of linked actions in response to the stimuli. They are working harder for longer, ideally showing a clear beginning, middle and end to their sequence.

○ **Reflecting and making comments** – pupils describe what they and others have done; say what they liked about a performance; give an opinion on how it might be improved; and then make practical use of such reflection to plan again to improve. The key features of an activity can be seen and copied because we remember what we see.

Achievement and progression

The Physical Education curriculum should enable all pupils to benefit and achieve. All children are entitled to be told how they have achieved, and to have their attainment assessed in a way that guides their future learning and progress.

Three headings serve to summarise the areas within which we want our pupils to achieve within the framework of the NC:

○ **Planning** thoughtfully precedes the performance as the pupil thinks ahead to what his or her response will be, trying to 'see' the intended outcome. Evidence of satisfactory planning can be seen in:

   a   good decision-making and thinking ahead with appropriate actions

   b   sensible, safe judgements

   c   good understanding of what was asked for

   d   a willingness to listen to and adapt to others' views

   e   an understanding of the elements that enhance quality, variety and contrast in 'movement'

   f   the expression of positive personal qualities such as optimism, enthusiasm, and a capacity for hard work in pursuit of improvement.

○ **Performing and improving performance** successfully is the main aim. In a satisfactory performance a pupil demonstrates:

   a   well-controlled, neat and accurate work

   b   the ability to practise to improve skilfulness

   c   the ability to perform skills safely

   d   whole-hearted and vigorous activity, sharing the space sensibly and unselfishly, with a concern for own and others' safety

   e   the ability to link actions together with control

   f   a capacity for skilfulness, variety and versatility

   g   pleasure from participating enthusiastically and confidently.

○ **Evaluating and reflecting** by the observant teacher, by oneself, and by pupils after observing a demonstration, help to inspire and guide pupils as they adapt, alter, develop and improve their work. Friendly, helpful, positive comments encourage and uplift the performer, and the observers benefit from the comments and guidance given. Where standards in evaluating are satisfactory, pupils can:

   a   see and identify the different actions taking place

   b   describe the most important features

   c   express pleasure at the part of the performance they liked

   d   comment on the accuracy and success of the work

   e   reflect sensitively with a concern for another's feelings

   f   suggest ways to bring about an improvement

   g   self-evaluate and act upon their own reflections.

Year 3 Gymnastic Activities programme

Pupils should be able to:

Autumn	Spring	Summer
1 Behave properly and dress sensibly.	**1** Practise, refine and adapt basic activities of jumping, rolling, climbing, swinging, balancing, and taking weight on hands.	**1** Display greater control and neatness in basic actions.
2 Work quietly and almost non-stop.		**2** Respond to a variety of tasks by planning, refining and adapting performance.
3 Respond immediately to instruction.	**2** Link together short series of actions on floor and on apparatus, with poised beginnings, middles and ends.	**3** Link movements in a logical sequence that can be repeated and enhanced with contrasts of shape, speed and good use of space.
4 Work hard to improve.	**3** Respond imaginatively to challenges – 'Can you...?'	
5 Share space sensibly and unselfishly, concerned for own and others' safety.	**4** Balance on varied supporting body parts at different levels.	**4** Apply the right amount of effort in jumps, rolls and balances for efficient performances.
6 Lift, carry and place apparatus sensibly.	**5** Demonstrate shape awareness by interesting use in sequences.	**5** Learn simple, traditional gymnastic skills such as rolls, balances and vaults.
7 Move neatly with good control.	**6** Make appropriate decisions quickly in planning thoughtful responses.	**6** Work co-operatively with a partner, learning sequences not possible alone.
8 Learn safe practice skills such as 'squashy' landings; keeping arms straight with head looking forwards when inverted on hands; putting thumbs under bars of climbing frames for a safe, strong grip.	**7** Work vigorously, inspiring deep breathing and perspiration.	**7** Recognise the value of contrasts in making work look more interesting.
9 Travel slowly on hands and feet, showing clear, thoughtful actions, on floor and on apparatus.	**8** Co-operate with a partner to create own sequences.	**8** Sustain energetic activity for longer periods.
10 Show good control in running, jumping, landing, and be able to adapt to the space available and to others.	**9** Try hard to develop performance.	**9** Observe others performing and suggest ways in which they might improve.
11 Show variety in running, jumping, landing, aware of feet, leg and arm actions at take-off, in flight and on balanced landings.	**10** Understand the contribution of shape to quality and variety and maintain good posture always.	**10** Give an impression of whole-hearted, enthusiastic participation at all times.
12 Show body-parts awareness in jumps, landing, climbing and balancing.	**11** Be instantly adaptable in sharing space with and being considerate towards others.	
13 Understand body shapes – long, wide, curled, arched, twisted.	**12** Demonstrate understanding through physical responses.	
14 Link a series of simple actions and be able and keen to repeat it.	**13** Demonstrate enthusiastically and comment readily on good features of others' performances.	
15 Observe others' actions and answer questions on what was seen.		

Lesson Plan 1 • 30 minutes
September

At the start of the year the lesson's main emphases include: *(a) creating a safe, quiet, co-operative environment where all work together sensibly and unselfishly, particularly in sharing space. (b) establishing a tradition of immediate responses to instructions. (c) co-operating with others to lift, carry, assemble, share and then put away the apparatus.*

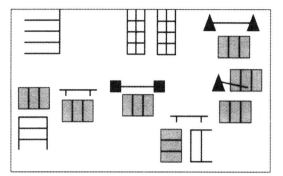

Gymnastic Activities

Floorwork
12 minutes

Legs

1 Show me your best running, keeping well away from others. When I call 'Stop!' stand in a space by yourself, not near anyone or any of the apparatus at the sides and ends. Stop!

2 Visit every part of the room, the sides, ends and the middle. Remember that good running is quiet and you don't follow anyone. Stop!

Body

1 Just where you are, show me a big high jump with a strong swing up in your arms and a nice, 'squashy' landing, softly on both feet, by letting your ankles, knees and hips 'give'.

2 Can you contrast the firm, strong stretch up with the more gentle, light and 'easy' actions in your landings?

Arms

1 Look for a space, then move, travelling slowly on hands and feet. Can you show me your travelling actions clearly?

2 Hands can travel by themselves, then feet by themselves, or they can all work together.

Apparatus Work
16 minutes

1 Travel to all parts of the room without touching any apparatus other than mats. When I call 'Stop!' show me a fully stretched body shape on the nearest piece of apparatus. Stop!

2 When I call 'Stop!' next time, can you show me your stretch on a different body part on a different piece of apparatus? Stop!

3 Now use your feet only to show me how you can get on to, along and then away from the apparatus.

4 Use hands and feet both on the apparatus and the floor in between to show me some of your favourite ways to travel.

5 Return to your number one apparatus places, ready to put away the same apparatus that you brought out.

6 Quietly, carefully and sensibly, please put your apparatus back to its position around the sides and ends of the room.

Final Floor Activity
2 minutes

Once again, show me your best running where you follow no-one and where you visit all parts of the room.

Teaching notes and NC guidance
Development over 4 lessons

NC elements being emphasised:

a   Being taught to be physically active.
b   Working safely, alone and with others.

Floorwork

Legs

1   For 'best running', ask for lifting of heels, knees, arms and head for lightness and quietness. The 'Stop!' gives practice in making immediate response.

2   Ask for straight line running to counter the curving, anti-clockwise running, common among primary school pupils, with all following and impeding all.

Body

1   In the air, stretch everything from arms above head right down to toes and ankles pointing. This contrasts with the 'give' in those joints for a soft, quiet landing.

2   Ankles are often under exercised with little mobility resulting. 'Really push with your feet and drive hard to stretch your ankles fully at take-off and in the air.'

Arms

1   Travelling should be done slowly to show the actions clearly and exercise the parts strongly. No quick scampering!

2   In addition to the usual head first with tummy towards the floor travelling, we can lead with feet or one side, and we can travel with back, front or side towards the floor.

Apparatus Work

(Preceded by teacher's 'Please go to your number one apparatus places.' Then 'Quietly and sensibly, please bring out your apparatus.')

1   Circulation is to 'all parts of the room, along straight lines, never following anyone and listening for my signal to stop.'

2   Stopping and showing a fully stretched body on the nearest apparatus is an exercise in listening and responding immediately.

3   'Feet only' means easy steps, jumps, swings on to apparatus; then steps, runs, jumps or bounces along and from. Ropes are not used because they need hands. Use of climbing frames is limited.

4   Hands and feet travel on floor and apparatus includes going on, under, around, across; gripping, pulling, circling, climbing, rolling and vaulting on narrow, wide, low, high.

Final Floor Activity

The class should be asked to 'Feel the lifting in your knees and heels for quietness. Pretend you have chalk on your feet and leave your straight line footprints all over the space.'

Lesson Plan 2 • 30 minutes
October

Theme: *(a) Neat, controlled, natural activities. (b) Body parts awareness; understanding of how body propels/ receives/supports body weight.*

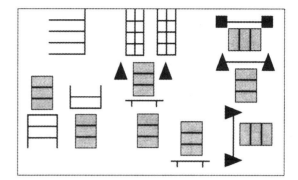

Floorwork
12 minutes

Legs

1 Practise quiet, soft upward jumps on the spot. Show me a good stretch in your ankles when you push up, and let ankles and knees 'give' on landing.

2 Now walk or run carefully a few steps until you see a good space, then show me another upward jump and soft landing.

3 Show me other favourite ways to travel, using feet only.

Body

1 Different parts of your body can support you as you move. Start off on your seat and show me how you can change from part to part (e.g. from seat roll to back; twist or roll on to tummy; curl to kneeling; to side falling on one hand, one foot).

2 Can you 'feel' the different actions you are using to move?

Arms

1 As you travel slowly using hands and feet, can you include moments when all the weight is on your hands?

2 Try to use hands and feet equally; hands, then feet alternately; and try hands and feet wide, then close together.

Apparatus
16 minutes

1 Use neat feet actions only as you travel to all parts of room, without touching any apparatus. Can you travel without stopping by using different actions to suit where you are?

2 You can walk when you have to go slowly under, through, across; run when there is clear floor; and jump over low apparatus such as mats, benches and planks. Can you show me any other favourite ways to travel, using feet only, and not touching apparatus?

3 Using feet or feet and hands, change now to travelling up to, on, along, then from the apparatus. Travel slowly to show me your actions clearly. As well as moving from apparatus to apparatus, can you think of the varied actions it is possible to include? (For instance, climbing; circling; hanging; rolling; sliding; balancing; springing; pulling.)

4 For a change, can you try some travelling on body parts other than, or in addition to hands and feet? A balance with a move to a new balance is a good way to practise (e.g. on seat; rock back to shoulders; twist legs back over one shoulder on to kneeling; roll sideways, back to sitting).

Final Floor Activity
2 minutes

Walk, run, jump with a nicely stretched body, then land silently by letting your legs 'give'. Be still for a moment, then start again.

Teaching notes and NC guidance
Development over 4 lessons

NC elements being emphasised:

a Exploring different means of taking weight on hands, and jumping.
b Responding readily to instructions.

Floorwork

Legs

1 Feel the body tension from top of head right down to strongly stretched ankles in the jump, and then the contrasting, relaxed, 'giving' in knees, ankles and hips on landing.

2 'A few steps' only, because the jumping and landing are the important parts. They can try one- and two-footed take-offs.

3 Teacher commentary will identify the class repertoire to spread the range of activities being used.

Body

1 Body parts travelling is more unusual and difficult than travelling on feet or hands and feet. Much experimentation and good use of demonstrations are needed.

2 Linking movements to be 'felt' include rolling, leaning, sitting, lowering, twisting, rocking, springing, tilting.

Arms

1 Once again, teacher commentary will identify the many ways to travel, slowly, on hands and feet. 'Crawling; one side then the other; hands only, then feet only; bunny jump; cartwheel; wide hands and feet; close hands and feet; hand-walking.'

2 They can bounce up and down on all fours, equally. Hands and feet alternately in cartwheels. Hands and feet wide for a difficult, strong action. Hands and feet close for a high, arching travel.

Apparatus work

1 Non-stop action with lots of running in open spaces; jumping over mats, across mats, benches and low planks; walking in congested, difficult areas; and own favourite extras.

2 The emphasis is on negotiating apparatus without touching any yet, and looking ahead to find quiet places.

3 Feet, or feet and hands to bring you on; hands or hands and feet to travel on, around, across, below, climb up, roll on or around; then a neat spring off. Ask them to think of all the words that describe their many and varied actions. Good demonstrations by a versatile trio or quartet can be used to elicit lots of action words. 'Observers, put your hand up as a signal that you can name four different actions in these excellent demonstrations.'

4 Travelling on many body parts, practised earlier in the floorwork, should inspire rocking and rolling on the back, spinning on the seat, twisting and rolling on the whole stretched, lying body and twisting over on the shoulders.

Final Floor Activity

A series of three, linked actions with the emphasis on body shape, and good still, starting and finishing positions. 'Land and be still. Look for a new space where you will not disturb anyone, and off you go again.'

Lesson Plan 3 • 30 minutes
November

Theme: *Body shape awareness in held positions and on the move. Awareness of long, wide, curled or twisted shapes within own performances and those of others. Shape's contribution to good style, efficiency of movements, and strong work.*

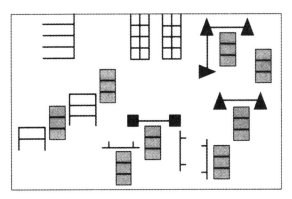

Floorwork
12 minutes

Legs

1 After a neat, still, tall start, walk, run and jump up into a beautifully stretched position. Land softly and show stillness again in a tall, stretched body position.

2 You can take off from one or both feet, and you can land on alternate or both feet. Landing one foot after the other helps you to slow down and control the whole landing.

3 Where are your arms on landing to help your balance? Try a sideways and a forward stretch of both arms.

Body

1 Using different body supporting parts, can you change from wide stretches to tight curls? (e.g. from standing, feet and arms stretched wide; to crouched position, with feet close together; to back lying with arms and legs wide; to curled small on shoulders, hands clasped under knees; to a long roll forwards on to wide hands and feet, etc.)

2 Can you plan and practise a little sequence of slow, almost non-stop movements?

Arms

1 Practise 'bunny jumps' with arms straight, legs kept bent.

2 For a contrast, can you lift your feet in the air, legs stretched, on one, two or alternate hands?

Apparatus Work
16 minutes

1 Run in and out of all the apparatus, but don't touch any until I say 'Stop!' Then show me a clear body shape on the nearest piece of apparatus. Stop!

2 Next time, when I signal, try to show me a body shape that contrasts with the others who are sharing your apparatus. Stop!

3 Can you travel up to a piece of apparatus and arrive on it with your body curled? Travel on the different surfaces and include contrasting body shapes as you go. Leave your apparatus and show me a beautifully stretched, still body before moving off to your next piece of apparatus.

4 Stay at your present piece of apparatus with no more than four others. Start and finish in a still, stretched position on the floor away from apparatus. Within your travelling on floor and apparatus, can you plan to include:

a a run and jump
b a variety of shapes as you travel
c weight on hands somewhere?

Final Floor Activity
2 minutes

Can you travel all around with a leg or legs sometimes stretched?

Teaching notes and NC guidance
Development over 4 lessons

NC elements being emphasised:

a Demonstrating changes of shape through gymnastic actions.
b Making judgements of performance and suggesting ways to improve.

Floorwork

Legs

1 The 'beautifully stretched' position in flight extends from long, upstretched arms above head, all the way down to the fully and strongly extended ankles. This clear shape looks good and is hard work compared with a limp, lazy, sagging performance.

2 The emphasis moves to how the feet are operating. A two-footed take-off helps an upward jump (one foot helps a long jump) and the alternate foot landing is the best for a gradual, slow landing.

3 Like the long pole of a tight-rope walker, the stretched arms help us to maintain our balance in landing.

Body

1 The linking movements between the stretches and the curls are important. Pupils need to be aware of rolling, rocking, lowering, springing up, twisting, sitting, lying, arching, upending, levering.

2 Three movements are sufficient for interest and as a challenge. Also of interest are different levels as we stand, sit, lie, arch, become upended.

Arms

1 In bunny jumps, keep the arms straight for strength and safety, legs bent for a quick lift up, and head looking forwards so that everything appears the right way up. Perfection is a straight line through shoulders, hips and hands, with fingers pointing forwards.

2 We start the bunny jump from a crouched position on hands and feet. The 'legs stretched' activities will start from standing with a swing up forwards to handstand or sideways into cartwheels.

Apparatus Work

1 Whole body should be involved in the 'clear body shape', where we encourage a variety of supporting parts, not always the feet.

2 Those with whom you are contrasting do not always know of this contrasting relationship. They might be relating to another.

3 In travelling through contrasting shapes on the apparatus, try to recall some of the linked actions on the floor, earlier.

4 In the last apparatus sequence requested, the 'weight on hands' can come at start on floor. 'Run and jump' can be at the end, coming away from apparatus. Curling to stretching is an easy way to travel on, around, along, under or across apparatus.

Final Floor Activity

One or both legs stretched while stepping, leaping up or forwards, jumping to turn in the air, slipping sideways with an upward lift, bouncing, travelling with a full stretch in flight.

Lesson Plan 4 • 30 minutes
December

Theme: *Space awareness and knowing where you and others are going as you share the floor and apparatus space, together. (b) Using own and general space, with different directions, levels and pathways to improve the variety and quality of the work.*

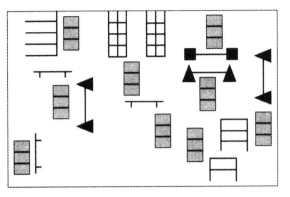

Floorwork
12 minutes

Legs

1 In your own, small space, can you run with high knee raising? Then show me normal running, using the whole floor space.

2 Can you add a little pathway, such as a circle, oval or figure 8, in your space, then repeat that pathway in the whole room space?

Body

1 Can you travel at different levels, and even in different directions, by bringing parts of your body together, then taking them apart? (e.g. back lying, legs and arms wide; close legs and arms, roll long body sideways on to back again; curl in small, hands clasped under knees; rock back on to stretched shoulder balance, legs apart; long rock forwards to standing, etc.)

2 Plan a short sequence to include each of the three levels.

Arms

1 This half of the class will travel on feet and hands along straight line pathways, with a stretched body for most of the time. The other half will travel, on feet and hands also, along curving or rounded pathways and you will try to bring parts of your body together and take them apart as you travel.

2 Remember that you can have your back, front or one side towards the floor, and you can lead with parts other than head.

Apparatus Work
16 minutes

1 Travel freely on floor and all apparatus, and include a direction change, either at start, finish, or within your travelling on the apparatus.

2 Show me how you can approach each piece of apparatus, going forwards, and leave it, facing sideways or, very carefully, backwards.

3 Can you try to include different levels at which you can travel or hold a still position, on apparatus and floor? (For example, high, standing on a box; medium, arched on a plank; low, body close to a bench or box.)

Final Floor Activity
2 minutes

Make a pattern of jumping where you include movement on the spot and either forwards, sideways, backwards or diagonally.

Teaching notes and NC guidance
Development over 4 lessons

NC elements being emphasised:

a Practising, developing, refining and repeating a longer series of actions, making increasingly complex movement sequences on the floor and apparatus.

b Demonstrating changes of direction and level through gymnastic actions.

Floorwork

Legs

1 An exercise in using own, personal space and the general, whole room space. In own space, upright body, with knees up to waist high and ankles pointed down, for about 8 counts, alternate with a circuit of the room back to own space.

2 Demonstrate with good performers, asking the observers to 'Look out for and tell me which pathways were very clear.'

Body

1 Try to include the more difficult high and medium levels, in addition to the easier low level. (High cartwheel from standing, feet and hands together into the star shape travel, feet and hands wide; leaping from feet together into one foot after the other. Medium travel on straight arms and legs, travelling arms only, then feet only, arching then flattening.)

2 For example – high cartwheel, opening and closing arms and legs; medium hands and feet, alternately arching and spreading hands and feet; low curl on back alternate with stretch and roll sideways.

Arms

1 A 'mostly stretched body' can be cartwheels, handwalking, long straight arms and legs crouched travelling, bouncing along on all fours with body long and straight. 'Body parts coming together and parting' can be crouched, hands only travel then jump feet to catch up, or walk arms forwards only, then walk feet forwards only.

2 Unless the teacher suggests it, or demonstrates otherwise, most will always travel with body towards floor and head leading.

Apparatus Work

1 Direction changes can include: steps and jumps forwards and sideways; rolls forwards, sideways and backwards; hanging and travelling sideways and backwards; hands on to vault on facing forwards and come off facing backwards or sideways; on hands and feet easily facing in all directions.

2 A momentary stay on apparatus, concerned principally with the immediate arrival and the departure. 'On, going forwards' includes steps, jumps, swings, rolls, levering off as in bunny jump with a twist to side.

3 High level, often on feet or hanging from arms, stretched, plus high jumps; medium, crab arched, or horizontal balance on one foot or across a bar; low, near to surface travelled on.

Final Floor Activity

A triangular pattern can include four skip jumps on the spot, then four diagonally forwards, then four diagonally backwards, then four to side and back to starting place.

Year 3

Lesson Plan 5 • 30 minutes
January

Theme: *Jumping, rolling, balancing.*

Floorwork
12 minutes

Legs

1 Do small jumps where you are. Keep your body straight, but let your knees bend to make the landing soft and quiet.

2 Using a very short run, go around the room, jumping up from one or both feet. Body straight in the air, and a nice 'squashy' landing, with a good bend in your knees.

3 Use stretched arms to help your balanced landing. Arms can stretch forwards, sideways or straight upwards.

Body

1 Lie on your back, curled up small, and roll back and forwards from seat all the way to your shoulders and hands.

2 Now, with hands clasped under knees, still curled up on your back, can you roll from side to side?

3 Can you start, crouched; lower into a roll back and forwards: roll from side to side; then rock back and strongly forwards and up on to feet?

Arms

1 With a long swing of arms from above head, can you try to balance on your hands?

2 Try an elbow balance. From a crouch position with feet apart, place hands on floor, shoulder width apart and under shoulders. Bend elbows slightly to place them inside and under knees. Tilt body weight forwards from feet.

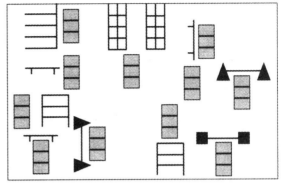

Floor sequence

Plan and practise a jump on the spot; run and high jump with a well balanced landing; lower down on to seat; roll back and strongly forwards back to standing; swing up on to hands or finish with an elbow balance.

Apparatus Work
16 minutes

1 As you travel all around the room without touching apparatus, can you include jumps across mats, over benches and low planks?

2 When I call 'Stop!' show me a balance on the nearest piece of apparatus, or apparatus and floor. Stop!

3 Travel freely on floor and apparatus. You may roll on mats, and from apparatus. With a nicely stretched body, can you jump off the apparatus, land softly, and lower into a smooth sideways roll?

4 Now stay at your present piece of apparatus to practise, repeat and improve the following:

   a start and finish on the floor, away from the apparatus
   b travel up to, on, along and away from your apparatus and show me...
   c jumps, rolls and, somewhere, a beautifully still balance with a clear body shape.

Final Floor Activity
2 minutes

Balance on tiptoes with arms stretched. Run, jump and land with a well-balanced finish, with straight arms again helping your balance.

Teaching notes and NC guidance
Development over 4 lessons

NC elements being emphasised:

a Exploring different means of rolling, jumping and balancing.
b Making appropriate decisions quickly and planning responses.

Floorwork

Legs

1 The jumps on the spot should be quiet with ankles and knees 'giving' like springs to absorb the shock. Ankles are often weak and underused and full stretches of ankles need to be pursued, with lots of practice.

2 The body tension in the air, with firmness felt throughout, is in contrast to the more giving, gentle feeling on landing.

3 If jump tends to be high, arms stretched sideways helps the balance. If jump is long, arms forwards helps the balance.

Body

1 The short rock back on to hands is like the start of a backward roll. The push forwards with hands is like the end of a forward roll. In both, keep well rounded with head on chest.

2 In side to side rolls, with hands tightly clasped under knees, feel the swing of legs and hands to start the rolling actions.

3 The lower, roll back and forwards is an easy movement. The roll sideways is an easy movement. The rock back to a strong push with hands and the rock up on to feet is the hardest movement.

Arms

1 Arms are straight for a safe, strong support. The head faces forwards because looking back under arms makes everything appear to be upside down. Feet together in the handstand is difficult to hold. It is easier to balance with one leg ahead, one back, making a long, low, straight line, like a tightrope walker's pole.

2 The difficulty here is to hold the slight bend in the elbows. Keep the bend as slight as possible or arms give too easily.

Apparatus Work

1 There will be simple, low jumps over part of a mat; higher jumps over benches and low planks; and there can be bounding, two-footed jumps along the length of a bench or plank.

2 'Balance' means that your body is on some small or unusual body support and not wobbling, which it wants to do.

3 The full forward rolls which will happen should have the head tucked well under so that arms, then shoulders and back receive the body (not the head), by a gradual bending of the arms.

4 The final apparatus sequence of jumping, rolling and balancing has an attractive variety of explosive, energetic jumps, smooth, flowing rolls, and still, firm balance. With a group sharing the apparatus, working almost non-stop, this can be very exciting to take part in, and to observe as a group demonstration.

Final Floor Activity

From balanced, still start to balanced, still finish will be only a few metres, being careful not to intrude on others' space. Deter long, long runs before the jumps.

Lesson Plan 6 • 30 minutes
February

Theme: *Sequences, and planning to link together a short series of actions on floor and apparatus with poised beginnings, middles and ends.*

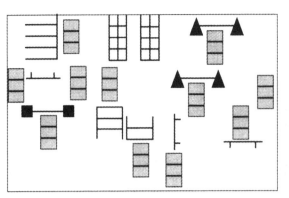

Floorwork
12 minutes

Legs

1 Using your legs, plan to show me a triangle of movements, starting and finishing at the same place on the floor.

2 Can you include three different actions in your travelling, take-offs or landings?

3 Emphasise clear, firm body shapes throughout. No sagging!

Body

1 In your own floor space, can you plan a short sequence of some of your favourite balances?

2 Can you plan to include varied supporting parts?

3 Working at different levels looks particularly good.

Arms

1 Slowly and quietly, travel on hands and feet.

2 Think about the actions you are doing and try to include at least three that are contrasting (e.g. cartwheel; on all fours with stretched arms and legs; hands first, then legs with a twist).

Apparatus Work
16 minutes

1 As you visit each different set of apparatus in turn, can you repeat a pattern of travelling up to, on and off quickly to a finishing place on the floor? Your finishing place becomes your starting place for your next practice, using a different set of apparatus.

2 Now expand your sequence by including a balance and weight on hands, which can take place on apparatus, floor, or a combination of the two.

3 Now stay at your present group with no more than five others sharing, to plan, repeat, practise and improve the following sequence:

   a start and finish on the floor away from apparatus

   b include at least two ways of travelling on feet

   c include a firm, clear body shape within a balance, and

   d include hands and feet travelling, which can be on floor; along, across, around, under apparatus; or using both floor and apparatus.

Final Floor Activity
2 minutes

Practise again your triangle of leg activities and show me three different, clear, firm body shapes. Demonstrating the shapes while in flight is most spectacular, but you can also include them as part of your starting and finishing positions.

Teaching notes and NC guidance
Development over 4 lessons

NC elements being emphasised:

a Practising, adapting, improving and repeating longer and increasingly complex sequences of movement.

b Working vigorously to develop suppleness, strength, stamina and to exercise the heart and lungs strongly.

Floorwork

Legs

1 Establish your own triangle space, with 3-metre sides and small enough not to impede others.

2 Aim for variety and attractive contrast within the trio. This variety is evident in the nature of the actions and any take-offs and landings (e.g. from and to one, both or alternate feet).

3 Clear body shapes enhance the appearance and efficiency of the movements, and make our bodies work hard to achieve them.

Body

1 Done in own floor space, slowly and thoughtfully, focusing on how to link them together, with, ideally, the non-supporting parts stretching strongly.

2 You can be standing, sitting, kneeling, upended on shoulders, in a crab arch, or side on to floor on one hand and one foot.

3 High level can be on one foot or tiptoes; medium on one foot with body horizontal, on a difficult crab; low, near floor on elbow and hand, or sitting, feet and arms off floor.

Arms

1 A 'sequence' needs at least two different actions, neatly linked and able to be repeated.

2 'Contrasting' from varied actions of parts concerned; levels shown; body shape, changing or not; from parts towards floor, front, back or side; from parts leading, head, feet or one side.

Apparatus Work

1 Whole class, well spaced, can travel clockwise from a starting set of apparatus to the next one, practising a still beginning and end and a very short, snappy middle on to and from apparatus.

2 Check they understand meanings of 'expand' and making their sequences bigger now, by adding a balance and taking weight on hands. Still ask for clockwise movement, and still, well controlled starts and finishes, signifying 'I am about to start' and 'I am finished.'

3 We stay at the one set of apparatus to allow much repetition and improvement to take place. Much travelling on feet, probably at start and finish. What actions? Some hands and feet travelling, particularly on difficult surfaces. Above, below, across, around? At least one firm, clear body shape within a balance. How difficult can you make it and still be in control of yourself?

Final Floor Activity

The range of possible body shapes includes being long and stretched; wide, like a star, and stretched; curled and round; arched to front, side or rear; twisted, with one body part working against another.

Lesson Plan 7 • 30 minutes
March

Theme: *Body shape awareness in stillness and in movement, and understanding body shape's contribution to quality and making the work more demanding. Limp or sagging is lazy and unattractive.*

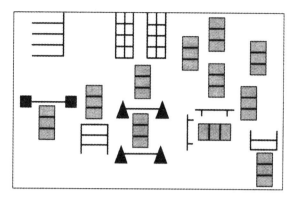

Floorwork
12 minutes

Legs

1 Can you travel with one or both legs sometimes stretched?

2 Stretching can take place in the air and during actions such as stretched leg walking, running, bouncing or slipping sideways.

Body

1 Can you show me three bridge-like shapes, neatly linked?

2 You can be high on feet or tiptoes; medium in a side towards floor position on one hand and one foot; and low in a sitting or arching position. Try to use different levels.

3 Try to be aware of the linking actions you are using – rolling, twisting, lowering, springing, levering, rocking, etc.

Arms

1 With hands on floor, can you jump your feet up into the air, kicking them past each other strongly? This can be called 'kicking horses'.

2 Try to keep your legs stretched as you kick them past each other. This action seems to help us to keep our balance.

Apparatus Work
16 minutes

Ropes
What body shapes can you show me using two ropes?

Climbing frames
Can you twist as you travel? Contrast this with a still scissors shape somewhere.

Mats
Practise again to improve your floorwork sequence of three bridge-like shapes, using mats to try more adventurous linking movements and bridges.

Trestles, pole, planks
Make bridge-like shapes on different parts of the apparatus, or apparatus and floor.

Box top, pyramid boxes and plank, mats
Try to work together as a group, moving from piece to piece of apparatus, holding a firm, clear shape which changes with your changing of places.

Box base, benches, mats
These low surfaces will allow much jumping and landing to take place. Show your clear shape in flight and try to contrast this held, firm shape with a moving body shape (e.g. a long, slow roll; a crouched 'bunny jump' across).

Final Floor Activity
2 minutes

Walk, run and jump, using your arms well and strongly to show me a clear body shape in the air – stretched, wide, long, curled, tucked or twisted.

Teaching notes and NC guidance
Development over 4 lessons

NC elements being emphasised:

a Emphasising changes of shape through gymnastic actions.

b Making judgements of performances and suggesting ways to improve.

Floorwork

Legs

1 Emphasise the 'travelling' and the 'sometimes stretched', as they experiment with both.

2 Stretching high within flight will include any long, wide sideways or front to rear extension of the legs (hurdling action). At a lower level we can stretch leg or legs as we walk, run, gallop, bounce, hop, hopscotch, skip or slip, opening and closing feet sideways.

Body

1 Ask class to identify examples of bridge-like shapes in the room to guide them, e.g. trestles, arch of ceiling, bench.

2 Bridge can be under, behind or to one side of the body, nearly always supported on two body parts, at least.

3 The linking movements should be done slowly as you transfer your weight from body parts to body parts, often involving an element of balancing.

Arms

1 In earlier lessons they will have practised bent leg bunny jumps, straight leg handstands, and split legs handstands, without the legs moving in the balance position.

2 As well as being another activity to practise while weight is on hands, the kicking back and forwards of both legs seems to help with the balancing.

Apparatus Work

Ropes

Climb two, stretching and curling, swing with body wide curled or tucked; circle around from standing back to standing.

Climbing frames

Twist by having a fixed point and working against it. Fix hands on bar, twist legs through space. Fix feet, twist upper body to pull to sitting.

Mats

Handstands, walk over into crab arch; and head-stand, tilt over into crab, are two more adventurous examples possible on mats.

Trestles

Bridges on feet on floor, hands against part of apparatus; on top of mat or plank surfaces; arched on pole.

Box, pyramid boxes and plank

Balancing group on many body parts on many apparatus parts. Leader of group sets rhythm for group.

    a Arrive on, move slowly into balance with strong, firm shape.

    b Slowly, move out of balance to next piece to repeat, ideally, on new body part with new clear shape.

Box, bench

Flight with a held shape. Then travel in contact with floor and/or apparatus in a shape that lets you travel, such as a roll.

Final Floor Activity

A triangle with short, 3-metre sides, to demonstrate shapes in flight, is attractive and interesting.

Year 3
Lesson Plan 8 • 30 minutes
April

Gymnastic Activities

Theme: *Partner work to: (a) provide new experiences not possible on one's own. (b) extend powers of observation, both of own and partner's choice of activities. (c) inspire enjoyable, desirable, co-operative social relationships.*

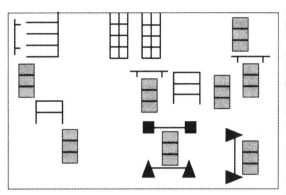

Floorwork
12 minutes

Legs

1   One partner will show the other a simple floor pattern of leg activities in own floor space.

2   Can you make your pattern of walking, running, jumping, skipping and any other activities short enough for your partner to copy and do along with you, in unison?

3   Now the other partner will lead in leg activities that use the whole floor space and return you both to your starting places.

4   Finally, combine the two sets of travelling without stopping in between.

Body

1   From a starting one leading, one following, can you build up to matching work in: from standing, sit curled small, rock back on to shoulders and hands, rock forwards through sitting back up to standing?

2   Variety can come from starting arms position in standing, from feet and leg positions throughout, and from your clear and changing body shapes.

Arms

1   Partner A makes various bridges supported on hands and feet. Partner B travels under and around the bridges, using hands and feet only.

2   Change over duties. Remember that you can have front, back or side towards the floor.

Apparatus Work
16 minutes

1   One leading, one following from a noted starting place on the floor. Travel up to each group of apparatus in turn and travel on it. Finish in your starting position. Now see if the following partner can remember where you went and all the ways of travelling that were used on floor and apparatus.

2   Show your partner a way of using hands to bring you on to a piece of apparatus. Now show your partner a way of leaving the apparatus where your feet are important. Travel around to the different pieces of apparatus.

3   Now stay at one piece of apparatus with your partner and no more than two couples. Can your pair plan, practise and work up to:

    a travelling from opposite sides up to, on, along, and from the apparatus in unison
    b including a balance, roll and a jump somewhere, and
    c finishing in your partner's starting position?

Final Floor Activity
2 minutes

Face partner. One leads in a simple jumping routine of feet opening and closing sideways and/or forwards to 4 or 8 counts.

Teaching notes and NC guidance
Development over 4 lessons

NC elements being emphasised:

a   Working safely, alone and with others.
b   Trying hard to consolidate performances.

Floorwork

Legs

1   Follower notes the actions and what the body parts are doing, first of all, e.g. stepping on tiptoes. Next, look for body shape, then any direction changes being used, e.g. tiptoe walking with high knees and straight arms, forwards, backwards and sideways.

2   Three actions are enough to observe and copy, at one time.

3   Leading partner will lead along straight lines, not curving, following along behind others.

4   Partners face each other on the spot, then follow around the whole room space, keeping about 2 metres apart for both.

Body

1   The changing levels, high standing, low sitting, medium on shoulders add an interesting contrast, as will slow, well-controlled, varied linking movements.

2   Long stretched standing to curled sitting to wide stretched on shoulders, with body working hard to show clear, firm shapes.

Arms

1   Holding, bridge making partner must give weaving partner plenty of room. Held positions vary from easy high on tiptoes with body arched to hard low, side on to floor, on one hand and one foot.

2   Feet and hand combinations include wide apart, close together, two and one, one and two, one and one, back, front or side to floor.

Apparatus Work

1   While leader has to plan where to go and what to include, the follower has to plan to observe... What actions and uses of body parts? What body shapes? What directions? At a more advanced level with a good class, they would also be considering... What effort? What speeds? What amounts of force?

2   'Hands on, feet off' means following at about 2–3 metres to give leader room, and to be able to observe efficiently. Leader going and waiting while follower catches up, might be helpful.

3   Partners now remain at the same apparatus setting to be able to 'repeat, adapt, improve and repeat a longer series of actions'. Three group places should be possible in one lesson for variety.

Final Floor Activity

Leading partner can quietly say the actions 'Side, in, side, in; left forward, right forward, left forward, right forward; side, in, side, in' as they perform their two part pattern.

Lesson Plan 9 • 30 minutes
May

Theme: *(a) Jumping, rolling and balancing. (b) Using right amount of effort for each task.*

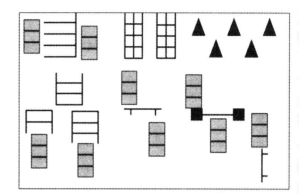

Floorwork
12 minutes

Legs

1 Balanced on tiptoes, stretch tall with arms and heels high. Use a short run into a space near you, jump up high, land with a soft squashy action, then lower to lying, curled up small. Roll sideways right over on to hands and feet. Return to balance standing on tiptoes and repeat.

2 Can you contrast your strong upward jump with a soft, quiet, slow lowering to back lying?

Body

1 Show me a 'firm' balance, where your whole body is working hard to show a clear shape with no wobbling. Now contrast this firmness with a relaxed, gentle moving on to another part or parts to balance strongly again.

2 How are you linking the balances? You can roll, curl, twist, lower, lever, spin, spring.

Arms

1 Try a long, slow swing of the arms from above your head up into a handstand. Balance is helped by letting one leg stay back and one reach forwards to make almost a straight line with your legs. (Like a tightrope walker's pole.)

2 Keep your arms straight and head facing well forwards.

Apparatus Work
16 minutes

Ropes
Can you join together a balanced starting position, a strong swing, and flowing roll to finish?

Climbing frames
Show me a balance on one frame, roll to other frame, and show me a second balance.

Benches
Show me contrasting ways to use the benches as springboards. For example, accelerate up to a vigorous drive from one, and a gentle push off and flowing action from the other. You may finish with a roll on the mats.

Trestle
Show me parts of the trestle on which you can hold a balance. After 2 or 3 seconds, change to a different part of you or your trestle to hold a new balance. Every time, make your shape firm and clear with your body working hard to keep this tension.

Pyramid boxes and bench
Start and finish, beautifully balanced, standing on the floor. Travel up to, on to, along or across your apparatus, and leave with a strong upward jump and landing, lowering into a sideways roll.

Boxes
As a group, demonstrate a variety of balances using mats, boxes, or boxes and mats. As a group also, can you vary levels, body shapes and supporting parts?

Final Floor Activity
2 minutes

Stand still, no fidgeting, but relaxed and with no body tension. Accelerate into an explosive leap and land in a strongly balanced position. Relax and repeat.

Teaching notes and NC guidance
Development over 4 lessons

NC elements being emphasised:

a Exploring different means of rolling, balancing and jumping.

b Emphasising changes of speed and effort.

Floorwork

Legs

1 Seven linked moves with the emphasis on running the parts together, sometimes smoothly and almost gently, sometimes firmly and with strength. Balance; run; jump; land; lower; roll; rise.

2 Contrast, like variety and repetition, is included among the aesthetic qualities of sequences, and is to be encouraged.

Body

1 The whole body must be involved in the 'firm', wide, long, arched, twisted or curled balance. Feel the difference as you relax and move out of balance.

2 Many demonstrations and much teacher commentary are needed to extend the class repertoire of travelling on body parts into each new held balance position. Such travelling/linking is less well practised than travelling on feet or hands and feet.

Arms

1 The split, near horizontal legs help the balance and needs to be demonstrated in case the class does not understand. Pushing foot hardly leaves the floor. Leading, kicking up foot travels a long way past the upturned body.

2 Straight arms tend not to give and collapse like bent ones. Head faces forwards, not back between hands which makes everything look upside down.

Apparatus Work

Ropes
Balanced start can be in contact with rope or not. Swing with hands together for strength. Land and roll.

Climbing frames
Balance can be with front, back or side towards frame, on seat, tummy, foot and hand, with many big body shapes.

Benches
Take-offs with one or both feet, with feet together or apart. Shape in flight a good contrast to final rolls.

Trestle
Balance on trestle, on trestle and floor, under trestle, on hands, hands and feet, seat, tummy, back, forearms.

Pyramid boxes and bench
Exciting, contrasting group. Be still; go; arrive and move along; fly; land and roll.

Boxes
Whole group must be aware of one another in action, even moving in and out of balance together, then changing to a new place for the next balance.

Final Floor Activity

Emphasise that we are demonstrating contrast which is an important, eye catching feature in any sequence.

Lesson Plan 10 • 30 minutes
June

Theme: *Direct teaching of simple gymnastic activities.*

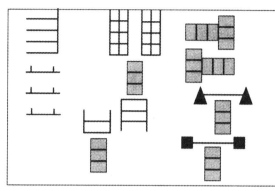

Floorwork
12 minutes

Legs

1   Do a stretched upward jump on the spot. Land and bounce to half the height of the first jump. Repeat. Now do four full upward jumps. 'Jump and bounce, jump and bounce, jump, 2, 3, 4.'

2   Can you do all of that again, but this time plan to add some direction changes?

Body

1   Horizontal balance standing on one leg with upper body leaning forwards to horizontal. Arms are stretched above head and other leg is stretched high behind so that arms, trunk and non-supporting leg make a long curving line.

2   Now lower to sitting in a 'V' position with legs straight and pointed upwards. Back is straight and arms help balance.

3   Now rock back to shoulder balance with legs and body stretched up and vertical. Hands and arms press down on to floor to assist balanced stretch.

4   With a long swing of legs and rock of body, return to standing, then horizontal standing to repeat.

Arms

1   Bunny jumps on the spot. With hands flat on floor, arms straight, hips and shoulders are lifted to a position above hands by a push up from feet. Knees are bent.

2   Cat spring is like a travelling bunny jump to reach forwards and support yourself on hands. From a crouched start, push whole body up and off floor a very short distance to land on hands with straight arms.

Apparatus Work
16 minutes

Ropes
Crossed feet grip. Try this from a standing position if strong enough, or from seated on a chair. Knees are apart and rope is gripped firmly under sole of one foot and above instep of other. Practise a small swing with arms straight, hands together.

Climbing frames
Start at bottom corner and climb up to top. Sit at top corner and come down diagonally, feet leading, to corner.

Mats
Forward rolls. Crouched start; hands on mat with head tucked in and chin on chest; push strongly with legs into roll keeping body tightly curled; heels come to floor near seat; reach forwards to finish in crouched position, ready to go again.

Inverted benches
Stand astride bench, mount to balance standing, one foot in front of the other.

Low boxes
Bunny jump on to end of box. Cat spring along box top. Bunny jump to twist down from box.

Trestles, pyramid boxes
Downward circle on low pole. Body starts balanced on pole on top of thighs with a strong hand grip and well stretched body. Bend arms and hips to let waist rest on pole. Curl slowly around pole with thumbs forward, fingers behind, until knees come under pole. Lower feet quietly to floor.

Final Floor Activity
2 minutes

Can you remember and repeat our opening jump, and do it once to each side of the room?

Teaching notes and NC guidance
Development over 4 lessons

NC elements being emphasised:

a Developing skill by exploring and making up activities.
b Trying hard to consolidate performance.

Floorwork

Legs

1 Stretch everything in the air, particularly the ankle joints which are seldom fully extended in everyday life. 'Give' softly on landing.

2 They can travel to one side or other, forwards or to rear, or they can make a quarter turn to face a different wall each time.

Body

1 Strong work for back and shoulder muscles, as well as the one leg holding the balance.

2 Slow, controlled lower to sitting with difficult, straight arms, legs and spine, all working hard against sagging and giving.

3 Ask 'Whose pointed feet and ankles are reaching up the highest towards the ceiling?' Body should be almost vertical over shoulders.

4 Strong arm swing and a bending of legs to tuck under you, are needed.

Arms

1 'Feel' strong with straight arms with hands pointing forwards for strength and efficiency. The ideal is to have hips above shoulders above hands, all in a vertical line.

2 In a cat spring, there is a moment when no body part is touching floor. The push up and forwards comes from stretching the bent legs.

Apparatus Work

Ropes

A good test for crossed foot grip is to take one hand off the rope during the swing to see if you can retain your foot grip.

Climbing frames

Keep thumbs under the bars, fingers over, for a safe, strong grip. Try to spiral or rotate down to next bar.

Mats

Two rolls in succession allows 'end of one action to become the beginning of the next.' At end of each roll, emphasise one push with hands, not two, from floor.

Inverted benches

In the balance standing position you can practise standing on one foot and moving other foot back and forwards, brushing side of bench before feeling for upper surface. This is how you feel your way forward, walking along the bench.

Low boxes

In bunny jumps you keep contact with floor. In cat springs there is a moment's flight with no contact with floor.

Trestles, pyramid boxes

Stress 'Thumbs forward' in circling down on pole, 'Head well in' in rolling forwards on to mat from sitting, kneeling or a low crouch at pyramid boxes and their plank.

Final Floor Activity

Jump and bounce; jump and bounce, jump, 2, 3, and turn.

Lesson Plan 11 • 30 minutes
July

Gymnastic Activities

Theme: *Partner work to: (a) make movements that you cannot do alone. (b) learn new activities from a partner. (c) recognise strengths and weaknesses of self and others and make allowances for them.*

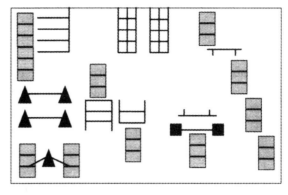

Floorwork
12 minutes

Legs

1 Follow the leader who will vary the work by using different parts of the foot, varied directions and more than one body shape.

2 New leader, can you take over and make your variety come from changing speed and adding on unusual arm and leg gestures?

Body

1 In a stretching and curling sequence, can one partner do a full body stretch, with the other partner copying? Now the second partner leads into a curled shape, copied by the other partner. Continue stretching and curling, leading alternately.

2 Can you work at different levels on a variety of supporting body parts?

Arms

1 Partner A observes B going from feet to hands and back to feet, in two or three ways. A then tells B what was good in the demonstration and includes one teaching point to bring about improvement.

2 After several repetitions, change duties.

Apparatus Work
16 minutes

Ropes
Using ropes and mats, build up to a matching sequence, done together.

Climbing frames
Can you show me ways that you can travel over, under and around each other?

Trestles, pole, planks
Start at opposite ends of the apparatus. Approach and pass each other to finish in your partner's starting place.

Bench, mats
Build up to a matching sequence, in unison, starting from opposite sides. Include a flight.

Boxes, mats, bench
Lead and follow on the same pathway, using floor and apparatus, using similar or contrasting actions.

Upturned bench, mats, boxes, plank
Can you keep some contact with your partner as you balance, travel, balance?

Final Floor Activity
2 minutes

Side by side, plan how you will run, jump and turn to face your starting place. Your turn can be in flight or on landing.

Teaching notes and NC guidance
Development over 4 lessons

NC elements being emphasised:

a Working safely, alone and with others.

b Exploring, improving and repeating a longer series of actions, making increasingly complex movement sequences.

c Making appropriate decisions quickly and planning responses.

Floorwork

Legs

1 Make the routine short enough to be able to remember and perform in unison. Follow at 2–3 metres so that follower can see actions and body shape clearly and easily.

2 New leader can develop existing routine with the change of speed and by addition of arm or leg gestures.

Body

1 Quick thinking and almost instant planning are needed to continue from partner's activity just seen. Keep going back to start to revise it, bit by bit.

2 High on feet; medium arched; low level stretching and curling travel of hands then feet.

Arms

1 Part complimentary observer, part coach and gentle critic, in the ideal one to one situation.

2 Observer looks for neatness with clear (not half-hearted) shapes, well-controlled, safe, strong arm work, obvious starting and finishing positions, and something original and personal about it.

Apparatus Work

Ropes
Plan, practise and build up your beginning, middle and end step by step.

Climbing frames
One can be stationary, one travelling; or they can continually be meeting and passing, on same or opposite sides.

Trestles
An exercise in 'negotiating' an obstacle, your partner, ideally with no contact.

Bench, mats
Decide on a starting signal, such as a heel raising by one. Check approach action, action and shape from bench, and the finish, landing in balance or rolling to a finish.

Boxes, bench
Leader goes and waits. Partner follows. This gives time to note the actions, shapes, directions for partner to match or to contrast.

Upturned bench, boxes, plank
Contact can be made by side by side travel, or one walking backwards holding other, or an assisted jump or lift.

Final Floor Activity

With a light hand hold at shoulder level, they can run side by side into a jump with a swing up of the same leg to twist to face where they came from. As they land, gently and slowly, side by side, the other hand can be joined at shoulder level, for the return to their starting places.

Dance

Introduction to Dance

This book aims to provide easy-to-understand, practical help for the non-specialist class teacher for whom the 1999 revised, further reduced version of the National Curriculum Physical Education document provides little practical help or specific guidance for the teaching of Dance.

The 'Teacher notes and NC guidance' that accompany each lesson plan aim to help teachers with main teaching points; summarise the main emphases; and explain what pupils should be achieving to satisfy good practice in Physical Education, generally, and in NC terms. Programme of Study, Attainment Target and Learning across the National Curriculum elements are translated into easily understood objectives appropriate for each Dance lesson.

This section aims to contribute to a sense of staffroom togetherness regarding why we teach Dance, what to teach in Dance, and how to teach Dance; provide a wide variety of stimuli as starting points to gain class interest, give a focus for attention and inspire a desire for movement; help teachers understand the content of Dance; and advise on a range of teaching methods designed to stimulate vigorous, enjoyable, physically challenging lessons that bring about pupils' achievement and progress.

The aims of Dance

Education has been described as the 'structuring of experiences in such a way as to bring about an increase in human capacity.' Dance aims to increase human capacity under the following headings:

1   **Physical development.** We focus on body action to develop neat, well-controlled, versatile movement. We want our pupils to move well and look poised, graceful and confident. The vigorous actions performed in Dance also promote healthy physical development, improving strength, suppleness and stamina.

2   **Knowledge and understanding.** Pupils learn and understand through the combination of physical activity (with its doing, feeling and experiencing of movement) and the mental processes of decision making, as they plan, refine, adapt, evaluate and then plan again for improvement.

3   **Artistic and aesthetic appreciation.** Gaining knowledge and understanding of the quality-enhancing elements of movement is a particular aim of Dance. Such understanding of quality, variety and contrast in the use of body action, shape, direction, size, speed and force is a major contributor to appreciation of good movement. We want our pupils to understand what is good about good movement.

4   **Creativity.** It has been said that 'If you have never created something, you have never experienced satisfaction.' Dance is a most satisfying activity, regularly challenging the pupil to plan and present something original. Opportunities abound for an observant, appreciative teacher to say, 'Thank you for your demonstration and your own, original way of doing the movements.'

5   **Expression and communication.** In Dance we communicate through the movement expression of the feeling or the action. We use, for example, stamping feet to express anger; we skip, punch the air or clap hands to show happiness; we swagger, head held high, to express self-assurance. Similarly, we create simple characters and stories by expressing them through movements associated with them. The old or young; rocket, machine or leaves; puppet, animal or circus clown, can all be expressed through their particular way of moving.

6   **Confidence and self-esteem.** Particularly at primary school, a good Physical Education that increases skill and recognises and praises achievement can enhance an individual's regard for him or herself, and help to improve confidence and self-esteem. Dance lessons are extremely visual and offer many opportunities for seeing improvement, success and creativity, and demonstrating these admirable achievements to others.

7   **Social development.** Friendly, co-operative social relationships are part of most junior school Dance lessons. Achievement, particularly in the 'dance climax' part of the lesson, is usually shared and enjoyed with a partner or a small group. Pupils also share space sensibly with others; take turns at working; demonstrate to and watch demonstrations by others; and make appreciative, helpful comments to demonstrators and partners.

8   **Enjoyment.** Dance is fun and an interesting, sociable, enjoyable physical activity.

9   **Eventual choice of lifestyle.** It is hoped that the teacher believes that enjoyable, sociable and physical activity, experienced regularly at school in Dance and other Physical Education lessons, generally, can have an influence on the pupils' eventual choice of lifestyle, long after they leave school.

Implications of aims for Dance teaching

1   Lessons will all have one thing in common – near continuous, enjoyable, vigorous physical activity. Lessons should be 'scenes of busy activity with everyone found working, not waiting'.

2   To justify the 'education' part of Physical Education, there must be opportunities to plan ahead thoughtfully to make decisions about actions. Pupils should also be encouraged to reflect on and comment on their own and others' actions and use these simple judgements to improve.

3   Pupils need to be helped to understand and use variety, contrasts and quality to develop their work. 'What actions? What uses of body parts? What shapes?' are the earliest questions. 'Where are you moving? Which directions and levels? On the spot or travelling?' are the next questions. 'How are you performing? Are your movements soft and gentle or firm and strong? Are you performing in almost slow motion or is your action explosive?' are questions associated with exciting, artistic, good-quality work with aesthetic appeal.

4   While there will always be much direct teaching and use of demonstrations to develop the class repertoire, there will also be much challenging to create original work. 'Show me how you can link these actions with a change of speed at some point.'

5   There will be much questioning of the class about the main features of the way we move to represent feelings, and about the particular way that inanimate objects or different types of people move, to guide pupils when asked to represent them through movement.

6   Pupils who work hard to achieve and improve should be recognised, praised and helped to feel good about themselves.

7   Partner work or small-group work should be a feature of most Dance lessons with pupils being brought closer together in a common endeavour.

8   In addition to the perspiration and deep breathing that vigorous physical activity inspires, there should often be smiling faces expressing enjoyment. When asked why they like something, a pupil's answer is usually 'It's fun!'

9   Class discussion should conclude that regular physical activity is good for you. It makes you look and feel better. It's sociable and it helps to make you feel relaxed and calm.

Teaching Dance

Dance is the hardest activity within Physical Education to teach because it requires the constant involvement of the teacher. A popular game can keep a class busy for long periods with little teacher input, while apparatus work in Gymnastic Activities inspires so many exciting, challenging actions that pupils can be kept busy, even if the teacher has little to say. Such 'ongoing potential' for minimum teacher involvement does not apply to Dance. A dance, once completed and presented, does not have the prolonged 'shelf life' of a game or gymnastic apparatus. Teacher and class have to move on, together, to their next, probably completely different dance.

We do not always need a story or a big theme as a starting point. Action words called out by the teacher, or seen on a card, can almost instantly get the class working because the task is so specific. The creative development should be equally clear, for example 'Make a short sequence using skip, stretch and turn in the order you choose.'

Everyone can use their imagination, but pupils need to be clear about what they are being asked to do and when to do it, when challenged to create more expressive sequences and patterns. Guidance must be specific. The teacher's task is to remove all vagueness and give the class an easily visualised, clearly understood image so that they know what they are doing. If pupils are set vague tasks, such as 'Find ways...' 'Make shapes...' or 'Explore levels...', they will not understand why they are finding, making or exploring, because there is no obvious end to it. Such a task is not specific enough and does not conjure up an easily visualised image. For example, 'Creeping and crawling' is much more purposeful if pupils are moving like a burglar about to enter a house. Balancing like a tightrope walker is much more interesting than being told to 'Travel slowly along a straight line.' Within the theme 'Nature', 'Explore being a butterfly' is far too loose and vague. Instead, we can look at the life cycle of the butterfly:

a   egg – all curled up as individuals
b   wiggling up and down like a caterpillar
c   into fluttering, flying butterfly, which can be represented by one or more dancers together, and then
d   it dies.

The dance has been given form and structure. Teacher and class have a clear picture in their heads; they know what to do, when to do it, and they know where the dance is going.

Teaching with 'pace'

Always high on the list of accolades for an excellent Dance lesson is the comment that 'It had excellent pace' and moved along, almost without stopping, from start to finish. Lesson pace is determined by the way that each of the several skills that make up the lesson is taught. A pattern for introducing, teaching and developing each of the several skills is helpful:

1. Move quickly into action. Using few words, explain the skill or task clearly and challenge the class to begin. 'Show me your best stepping, in time with the music. Begin!' This near-instant start is helped if the teacher works enthusiastically with the pupils.

2. Emphasise main teaching points one at a time while the class is working. The class all need to be working quietly if the teacher is to be heard. 'Visit all parts of the room, sides, ends and corners as well as the middle.' 'Travel along straight lines, never following anyone.' (Primary school pupils will always travel around in a big anti-clockwise circle, all following one another, unless taught otherwise.)

3. Identify and praise good work while the class is working. The teacher should not say 'Well done' without being specific and explaining what is considered to be praiseworthy. Comments are heard by all and remind the class of the key points. 'Well done, Emily. Your tiptoe stepping is lively and neat.' 'Tony, you keep finding good spaces to travel through. Well done.'

4. Teach for individual improvement while the class is working. 'Gary, swing arms and legs with more determination, please.' 'Ann, use your eyes each time you change direction to see where the best space is.'

5. Use a demonstration, briefly, to show good quality, variety, or a good example of what is expected and worth copying. 'Stop, please, and watch Cara, Michael, James and Christine step out firmly with neat, quiet footwork, never following anyone.' 'Stop, everyone, and watch how Julie is mixing bent, straight and swinging leg actions for variety.'

6. Very occasionally, to avoid using too much activity time, a short demonstration is followed by comments from observers. 'Half of the class will watch the other half. Look out for and tell me whose stepping is neat, lively and always well-spaced. Tell me if someone impresses you for another reason.' The class watch for about 12 seconds and three or four comments are listened to. For example, 'John is mixing tiny steps with big ones.' 'Mary is stepping with feet together, then with feet wide apart.' Halves are changed over and the process repeated.

7. Thanks are given to all the performers and to those who made helpful, friendly comments. Further practice takes place with reminders of the good things seen and commented on.

Awareness of 'movement'

The teacher's knowledgeable observation of the class in action is the starting point for all improvement and development. Helpful comments and teaching points made to individuals and the whole class should always be based on what has been observed. A pattern to follow, when looking at the several elements of movement, is a helpful guide:

1. What actions and uses of body parts are taking place? Are the actions being performed quietly, neatly, whole-heartedly, correctly and safely, always aware of others?

2. What body shapes are being clearly shown while moving and while still? We always have a body shape and we want pupils to know that it contributes to the appearance and efficiency of movements. Poor, lazy, limp, sagging shapes look unattractive and mean the body is not working hard. Firm, clear shapes need effort and look good.

3. Where are the actions taking place? Stage one, under this heading, will almost certainly involve the teacher stopping pupils all travelling around in an anti-clockwise circle. Good sharing of space for easy, safe practice; working in different directions and at different levels; and contrasting the use of own floor space with whole room space, all enhance the appearance of the work.

4. How are pupils moving? Effort and speed, like shapes, are ever-present features within an action and their conscious application is a major contributor to better-controlled, interesting, contrasting and better quality performance. How firm or gentle? How fast or slow? How soft or explosive? When a pupil consciously starts to contrast a lively, strong, upwards leap with its slower, softer landing, the movement awareness training is starting to show results.

5 How well do pupils 'select and combine their skills, techniques and ideas and apply them accurately and appropriately', a main requirement within the National Curriculum? Assessment of pupils' progress and achievement will be based on their ability to plan and link together a series of movements. The quality of the eventual created dance will be directly related to the quality of the teacher's powers of observation and his or her subsequent comments. His or her enthusiastic demands for the highest possible standards – the best and neatest actions; well-controlled use of body parts; firm, poised body shapes; good use of effort and speed – will all have been influenced by an awareness, through observation by the teacher, of what is happening and what needs to be improved.

A pattern for progressing, improving, and developing Dance movement

Stage 1: The What? (Concentrate on the body parts involved and the actions performed.)

What actions? Make the actions neater, better controlled and more correct – travelling, jumping, landing, rolling, balancing, turning, rising, falling, gesturing, being still, etc. (for example, 'Can you step quietly and neatly, visiting all parts of the room?')

What body parts? Ask for better posture, poise, body tension and an awareness of all the body parts concerned as pupils practise whole-heartedly to improve. The full range of movement in the joints concerned is used, displaying strength, suppleness and a good attitude. Neat and varied use of feet, legs, arms, hands, shoulders and head provides interesting and attractive variety. (For example, 'Which parts of your foot can support you? Heels, toes; insides or outsides; long or short steps or a mixture?')

What shapes? Improve 'body-parts awareness' with a feel for different shapes, making them strong, clear and firm, improving quality and variety. (For example, 'Step out nice and tall as you travel. Can you show me clear arms, legs and body shape? Are you long and stretched or is there a body shape change somewhere in your stepping?')

Stage 2: The Where? (Concentrate on the space being used, worked in and shared.)

Develop 'space awareness', with an understanding of the way that direction and level changes and the use of own and whole room space enhance the work and improve its quality and its variety, as well as letting the dancers practise to improve, undisturbed by others. (For example, 'Can you sometimes step on the spot, if you are in a crowded area, and sometimes use the whole floor space? Stepping actions, sideways and backwards, can be interesting and the free leg can swing in many directions.')

Stage 3: The How? (Concentrate on the amount of effort and speed being used.)

Develop an understanding of how 'firm and vigorous' or 'explosive and fast', for example, can contrast attractively and often surprisingly with 'soft and gentle' or 'gradually and slowly' to improve real and obvious contrast and variety. (For example, 'Within your stepping, can you include a change of speed? Slow, slow, quick, quick, slow, slow, for example. Can you make parts of your stepping small, soft, gentle, and make other parts bigger, firmer, stronger?')

Stage 4: The Performance

Work harder for longer, building longer, more complex sequences, ideally showing a clear beginning, middle and end to the sequences. In NC terms, the ability to improve, remember and link actions is something that pupils should be able to demonstrate. (For example, 'In your three- or four-part stepping sequence, can you include: (a) varied stepping actions; (b) interesting use of space; and (c) a change of speed somewhere?')

National Curriculum requirements for Dance – Key Stage 2: the main features

Programme of Study   Pupils should be taught to:

a create and perform dances using a range of movement patterns, including those from different times and cultures

b respond to a range of stimuli and accompaniment.

Attainment Targets   Pupils should be able to demonstrate that they can:

a link skills, techniques and ideas and apply them accurately and appropriately, showing precision, control and fluency

b compare and comment on skills, techniques and ideas used in others' work, and use this understanding to improve their own performance by modifying and refining skills and techniques.

Main NC Headings when considering progression and expectation

Planning – This provides the focus and the concentrated thinking necessary for an accurate performance. Where standards of planning are satisfactory, there is evidence of:

a the ability to think ahead, visualising what you want to achieve
b good decision-making, selecting the most appropriate choices
c a good understanding of what was asked for
d an understanding of the elements of quality, variety and contrast
e an unselfish willingness to listen to others' views and adapt own performance correspondingly.

Performing and improving performance – This is always the most important feature of a lesson. We are fortunate that the visual nature of Physical Education enables pupils' achievement to be easily seen, shared and judged. Where standards in performing are satisfactory, there is evidence of:

a successful, safe outcomes
b neat, accurate, 'correct' performances
c consistency, and the ability to repeat and remember
d economy of effort and making everything look 'easy'
e adaptability, making sudden adjustments as required.

Linking actions – With a view to getting pupils working harder for longer, which is a main aim for Physical Education teaching, encourage them to pursue near-continuous, vigorous and enjoyable action, expressed ideally in deep breathing, perspiration and smiling faces.

Reflecting and evaluating – These factors are important because they help both the performers and the observers with their further planning, preparation, adapting and improving. Where standards are satisfactory, there is evidence of:

a recognition of key features and keen and accurate observation
b awareness of accuracy of work
c helpful suggestions for improvement
d good self-evaluation and acting upon these reflections
e sensitive concern for another's feelings, and a good choice of words regarding another's work.

Year 3 Dance programme

Pupils should be able to:

Autumn	Spring	Summer
1 Listen and respond immediately to instructions. Use neat, quiet actions.	**1** Plan short, expressive performance based on winter words on cards, contrasting e.g. the rushing stream with the floating snowflake and spiky ice shapes with melting snow.	**1** Make dances with clear beginnings, middles and ends.
2 Dress sensibly and safely. Share floor space unselfishly and safely.	**2** Develop skill in basic travelling actions, keeping to the rhythm of accompanying music.	**2** Be given opportunities to work alone to develop own personal skill.
3 Work whole-heartedly, practising varied basic travelling actions and linking them into repeating patterns in time with music.	**3** Learn, and join creatively, folk dance figures for couples.	**3** Be given opportunities to work with a partner to share ideas and combine to make a bigger, more special dance.
4 Develop awareness of basic actions and of how body parts concerned are working – feet, legs, hands and trunk.	**4** Practise to improve, remember and be able to repeat patterns of movement.	**4** Learn an easy, traditional circle dance, listening and responding to the rhythm of the accompanying music.
5 Compose steps, hands and whole-body patterns and be able to repeat them.	**5** Learn a simple, traditional folk dance, co-operating with a partner and a team, learning about the good quality features involved.	**5** Compose and control movements by varying speed and tension. Develop in a partners 'Fast and Slow' dance.
6 Become body-shape aware. Understand how clear, firm shapes enhance the look of basic actions.	**6** Use body contact rhythmic sounds as a dance accompaniment and stimulus.	**6** Experience working with a variety of stimuli, including music.
7 Celebrate the seasonal 'Fireworks' with their varied starting shapes, contrasting actions and varied use of body tension and speed.	**7** Experience and be praised for planning and creating a dance.	**7** Express moods, ideas and feelings imaginatively through the body actions usually associated with them.
8 Plan and link skills and work hard to practise and improve them.	**8** Enrich movements by understanding and varying shape, direction, speed, level and body tension.	**8** Display increasing self-confidence, control and versatility, enthusiastically practising to improve and share achievements.
9 Celebrate Christmas in the 'Puppet Maker's Workshop', and experience the jerky, floppy, loose movements of puppets – plus the movements of their sad maker.	**9** Express identity of characters through body movements they use. Plan and practise repeating patterns of circus work actions.	**9** Comment on what they and others have just shown.
10 Observe demonstrations by partner and others and make helpful comments about what was admired.	**10** Recognise and describe a set of movement patterns.	

Lesson Plan 1 • 30 minutes
September

Theme: *Unselfish sharing of space; instant responses to instructions; neat, quiet, travelling actions.*

Warm-up Activities
5 minutes

1 Show me your best walking as you visit all parts of the room.

2 When I call 'Stop!', stop immediately... stop! If you are near anyone or anything, take one step away into your own space.

3 This time, walk along in a straight line, never following anyone. Swing your arms and step out smartly.

4 Stop! Be still in your own space, quickly.

5 Now show me your very best, quietest, neatest running, still in a straight line, never following anyone. Go!

6 Stop! Once again, let me see you all in a good space, not near anyone or anything (e.g. piano, wall, gymnastic apparatus).

Movement Skills Training
15 minutes

1 Stand in your good space where you can all see me. Join with me in some of the actions we can do on the spot.

2 Step with a good lift forwards in knees and front of foot. Swing your arms, 1, 2, 3, 4. Swing and step, lift your foot.

3 Like a boxer now, patter with a quick running action with feet hardly leaving the floor. Your arms stay by your sides and there is no lifting of your body. Your head stays where it is.

4 Skip now, lifting your whole body with each skip 'step – push; step – push; step – lift', and swing your arms strongly.

5 Bounce very softly, with toes hardly leaving the floor. Show me a good knee stretch as you go up, and a good knee bend as you land. Stretch, bend; stretch, bend; push, land; up, down.

6 Well done. You did those actions on the spot very quietly and very neatly. Now try them on the move as you travel to the ends, corners, sides and across the middle of the room, never following anyone. Go! Walk... quick patter... skip... bounce. Keep going!

7 When I call 'Stop!', stop immediately, and stand in your own big space... stop!

8 Well done. That was an excellent stop and I like your spacing.

Dance — Clever Feet
10 minutes

1 Often, when we travel in the hall, we come to a busy place with lots of others in the way. If that happens, we can keep moving by performing on the spot until there is enough room to carry on.

2 Let's practise a 'Clever Feet' dance. Do each action four times on the spot, followed by eight times while travelling. Let's try hard and do all four each time – stepping, pattering, skipping, bouncing. Start on the spot, pretending it's crowded. Go! Step on the spot, 3, 4; patter, patter, quickly for 4; skip and skip and skip for 4; bounce gently. Now we travel; step and travel, off you go, 5, 6, 7, now patter; patter, 2, 3, 4, quickly, quickly, now we skip; and skip and skip and travel, 5, 6, 7, now bounce; bouncing, 2, 3, 4, low and quiet, and start again.

3 Stop! Well done. You all kept going in time with the bouncy music. Let's look at demonstrations by each half of the class. Those who are watching can help by clapping for the four- and eight-count parts of our dance.

Dance

Teaching notes and NC guidance
Development over 2 lessons

Pupils should be taught to:

a **respond readily to instructions.** The lesson is full of direct teaching and specific instructions. The instruction to 'Stop!', 'Go!', and to join the eight different parts of the dance climax reveal the inattentive or badly behaved, who should be dealt with. The instant responders are praised. If they are also asked to demonstrate, their continued enthusiastic participation is assured;

b **be mindful of others.** Space awareness is practised in the warm-up to prevent the typical anti-clockwise travelling around the room, common in primary schools. The instruction 'Stop! Be still and in your own space, quickly' makes the pupils conscious of giving others good space to work in, as well as giving them an exercise in responding well;

c **recognise the safety risks of wearing inappropriate clothing, footwear and jewellery.** This, the first lesson with a new class, is the right time to establish the necessary traditions for the way that they will always dress (and behave and respond) in future Physical Education lessons. No watches, rings, necklaces; no long trousers that catch heels; no unbunched hair that impedes vision; no socks without shoes. Barefoot work is recommended because it is quiet, enhances the appearance of the work and enables the little-used muscles of the feet and ankles to develop as they grip, balance, propel and receive the body weight.

Warm-up Activities

1–6 While the class is 'best walking', the teacher is coaching for good spacing. 'Visit every part of the room, sides, ends, corners, as well as the middle.' On 'Stop!' they are told to take one step only into a space if they are too near anyone or any walls or apparatus. 'Never follow anyone. If they stop suddenly, you might bump into them.'

Movement Skills Training

1–8 The non-stop action of the warm-up continues as the teacher demonstrates and leads the class through steps, patters, skips and bounces, teaching to emphasise the main features of each, e.g. steps with 'good lift forwards in knees'; patter 'with feet hardly leaving the floor'; 'swing your arms strongly' in skipping; and 'good knee bend as you land' in bouncing, always with the frequent, attention-demanding 'Stop!' and 'Stand in your own big space.'

Clever Feet Dance

1 Marking time on the spot at a busy floor space is something pupils seldom do, until asked.

2 The a: b: c: d, four-part sequence of stepping, pattering, skipping and bouncing, all on the spot, is followed by a second four-part sequence, with the same actions, but travelling. On the bouncing, final part of the first sequence (all done in a good space), they will be looking for a good space to start their travelling sequence, unimpeded. The rhythm of the music, and the teacher's continuous commentary and reminder of the actions, keep the whole class together.

3 Demonstrations, where half of the class sit together at one end of the room to watch the other half performing, will be an ever-present feature and important part of the climax of Dance lessons and pupils' improvement. As well as being asked to 'help by clapping for the four- and eight-count parts of our dance,' observers are asked 'Please watch and then tell me which dancers you particularly liked and why.'

Lesson Plan 2 • 30 minutes
September/October

Theme: *Body parts awareness, particularly feet and hands.*

Warm-up Activities
5 minutes

1   Stand in your good space and clap hands to the music with its sets of eight beats. Clap, 2, 3, 4, 5, 6, 7, again.

2   This time, on counts seven and eight, smile and do a little, friendly wave to someone standing near you. 1, 2, 3, 4, 5, 6, friendly wave; 1, 2, 3, 4, 5, 6, smile and wave.

3   Still clapping, smiling and waving, walk around this friendly hall, meeting and greeting lots of others. Walk, 2, 3, 4, 5, 6, smile and wave; 1, 2, 3, 4, 5, 6, hello, hello.

4   Run or skip or bounce in and out of one another. Do not clap, but still look at and recognise someone near you on counts seven and eight. You might do counts seven and eight on the spot, like we practised in the last lesson. I will be looking at your neat, quiet actions.

Movement Skills Training
15 minutes

1   Let's give our legs a little rest while you show me some of the actions that our hands can do. Stretch... bend... shake... circle... click... clap, of course... come together, then come apart... point... slap and make sounds on the body.

2   Try some of these actions in different places, above head, to one side, to front, to rear.

3   Make hand sounds on different parts of your body and mix them with the sounds of clapping and clicking. Let me hear your steady rhythm. 1, 2, 3, 4; sound and sound and sound for 4.

4   Good. Can you join together three or four different hand actions? Keep a nice rhythm, 1, 2, 3, 4.

5   Change now to practising three or four travelling actions with your feet and legs. You can repeat the steps, bounces, skips and even the pattering of our previous lesson – or use other favourites of your own, e.g. hopscotch, glide, slide, leap, chasse. (Chasse is a step to the right with right foot, closing left foot to the right. Side, close; side, close.) Repeat each action eight times and let me see you using your eyes to look for good spaces. Ready? Begin.

Dance – Hands and Feet Patterns
10 minutes

1   Find a partner and number yourselves, one and two. Number one, go first and show each other your three- or four-part pattern of hand actions. Repeat each action four times.

2   Do it again so that your partner can remember it.

3   Now, with number two going first, show each other your three- or four-part pattern of travelling actions. Do your pattern two or three times to help your partner remember it.

4   Decide whose travelling actions will be used. The other's hand actions will be used. The music is playing for you to practise. Each time, the leader may quietly say the actions, as a reminder. Practise now, on the spot, then travelling.

5   Sit down at this end to look at three couples who are working well as partners. Tell me what you like about their hand actions and the way they travel together.

Dance

Teaching notes and NC guidance
Development over 3 lessons

Pupils should be taught to:

a **be physically active.** First and foremost, we want 'scenes of busy activity', with everyone working and no-one waiting. We also want our classes to enjoy the lessons and to understand near non-stop activity, learning lots of interesting activities, which will provide such enjoyment. Brief, easily understood instructions that inspire quick responses; lots of individual teaching and praise while the actions are happening; and an enthusiastic teacher who joins in as an example, are all contributors to a lesson's good pace;

b **respond readily (and whole-heartedly) to instructions.** We need to train pupils to respond immediately to fill as much of the lesson with activity as possible. We also want them to be whole-hearted, putting everything into their work as they use joints to their full limits; make shapes full and firm with no lazy sagging; and work hard to move quietly and under control.

Warm-up Activities

1-4 This start-of-year, sociable, good fun clapping, walking, smiling and waving start of lesson can be adapted as a seasonal warm-up for most of the year. The 'smile and wave' or 'Hello! Hello!' on counts 7 and 8 can become 'Happy Christmas!' 'Happy Birthday!' 'Happy Holidays!' or 'Happy New Year!'.

Movement Skills Training

1-4 In a 'body-parts awareness' lesson, pupils feel the many varied ways in which hand actions can enhance a whole body's movement, both in changing body shapes and in providing sound accompaniment. The triple challenge to reach into different spaces; make different hand sounds on body parts; and to 'keep a nice rhythm' will inspire varied responses for the teacher to praise, recognise and share through demonstrations to help everyone improve.

5 The class now practise a repeating sequence of three or four feet-and-legs travelling actions. A music accompaniment with an eight-count phrasing (as in many English and Scottish country dances) helps to give each action the correct length of time. In the previous month's lesson we set high standards of attentiveness, behaviour and spacing. In this lesson, as pupils travel using feet and legs, we need to insist on neat, quiet, 'correct', focused actions, because these travelling steps, jumps, bounces, skips, hopscotches, glides, and chasse steps will be continually used in Dance lessons. Pupils need to be told and shown what is good quality action.

Hands and Feet Patterns Dance

1 'Watch and remember your partner's three- or four-part sequence of hand actions' is a challenge to the performer to remember, and to the observer to watch and remember.

2 Each repeats his or her own sequence of hand actions, helped by the teacher's guidance. 'Are the actions different and do they include a contrast? For example, is there a small and a large? A firm and a gentle? One near the body and one reaching far out?'

3-5 After both demonstrate their travelling actions sequences, they decide which one to use. The other partner's hand actions sequence is used to complete their partner's dance. Each may quietly say the actions of their part as a helpful reminder. After the demonstrations with follow-up and encouraging comments, everyone practises again, trying to improve.

Lesson Plan 3 • 30 minutes
October

Theme: *Awareness of basic actions and contrasting body shapes.*

Warm-up Activities
5 minutes

1 With feet apart, reach up high with arms wide. Feel the strong, wide stretch right up to your finger tips.

2 Bring one foot in beside the other and bend right down until your back, knees and ankles are bent.

3 Move one foot to the side and stretch up wide again. Show me your beautiful, wide 'X' or star shape.

4 Slowly, continue bending low and stretching high and wide.

5 Lie on your back in a long, firm, stretched shape. Feel your toes reaching down and your hands reaching far above your head.

6 Bend both knees up, lift your head and back, and grasp hands around your knees. Slowly, continue lowering to a stretch shape and curling in to a rounded shape.

7 Try this stretching and curling while lying on one side and feel how your whole body is taking part.

8 Let's join all three stretchings and bendings, starting with the standing. (After the third bend, they sit and lie back, stretched. After the third stretch and bend on back, they roll over on to one side. After the third stretch and bend on side, they roll on to front and stand to repeat the three-part sequence.)

Movement Skills Training
15 minutes

1 Stand in lines of four, two boys and two girls, behind a leader. In 'The Snake', the leader's actions ripple down your snake's body as each person passes on the action. Keep one metre apart so that you can see the action of the person in front. Leader, show a clear action as you take your team away... go!

2 Keep repeating your neat, clear action, leaders. Are your feet together, apart, or passing each other?

3 Stop! Well done, leaders and teams. Most of you kept together well and looked for good spaces. Leader, go to the end of the snake. New leader, please give us a new action and try to make your body shape firm and clear. With the music... go!

4 Stop! Well done, leaders. I saw wide bouncing; tiptoes, stretched walking; and firm, stretched arms in skipping. Change again. New leader, try an interesting new action (e.g. slither, slide, chasse, hopscotch, swing leg across, to one side or behind). Go!

5 Stop! Thank you for those excellent travelling ideas that I saw rippling down your snakes. Change over and let the last leader come to the front. Last leader, you might try an action, mostly on the move, but sometimes on the spot. All ready? Go!

Dance – The Snake
10 minutes

Music: Any lively, jazzy, medium-to-fast tempo.

1 Snakes, I will call 'Change!' as the signal for the leaders to change. Leaders, travel carefully, always looking for good spaces. Snakes, keep together as your four actions ripple to your tail.

2 Stop! I will give each snake a number and ask each one, in turn, to demonstrate while all the other teams watch. Number one... two... three... four... everyone, go!

Dance

Teaching notes and NC guidance
Development over 3 lessons

Pupils should be taught to:

a **respond to music.** To help them feel the music's beat, the teacher can chant rhythmically. The medium-speed, bouncy music usually breaks down into phrases of eight bars. 'Travel, travel, 3, 4, neat actions, 7, 8; keep together, space out well, 5, 6, 7, 8; 1, 2, 3, 4, 5, 6, leaders change.' As well as keeping pupils with the music, such rhythmic accompaniment by the teacher can be used to improve the quality of the action. 'Softly, softly, into spaces, 5, 6, 7, 8; lively legs and swinging arms, 5, 6, 7, 8; bodies firm with nice strong shapes, 5, 6, 7, 8.'

b **control movements by varying shape and size.** By making each of the four leaders responsible for a new aspect of movement, the class is made aware of some of the features of movement that makes it interesting to perform and attractive to watch. Body shape variety with clear, firm use of body parts and small, neat, quiet movements contrasting, for example, with larger, livelier, more vigorous travelling movements, can be taught, experienced and understood.

Warm-up Activities

1–8 As well as being an excellent exercise, taking every joint to its full range, a long, high, strong, wide stretch from hands down to tiptoes, contrasts well with a curled, closed, rounded shape. The joined-up stretching and bending actions are practised within a joined-up sequence of three parts: standing; back lying; and lying on one side. Such linking of groups of actions neatly with good control and precision is an important requirement within the National Curriculum. The challenge 'Let's join all three stretchings and bendings' is a typical lead into a series of linked actions.

Movement Skills Training

1 A good start position is with all lines of snakes facing the teacher at one end of the room. A metre apart lets each one in the line see the actions of the one in front of them, as the actions ripple from the head down to the tail of the snake.

2 Before leaders take teams away, they are told 'Leaders, give your snake good spaces to travel through and try to include at least two actions. Do not rush ahead and lose your tail.'

3–5 Snakes are stopped to let a new leader come to the front and to let the teacher explain the new leader's different emphasis from clear actions and neat use of feet and body; to an emphasis on clear body shapes; to an awareness of spacing, which can include travelling to all parts of the room; moving on the spot; as well as going backwards or to one side.

The Snake Dance

1 While they perform, the teacher will call 'Change!' as the signal for the leader to drop to the end of the line to make space for a new leader and new emphasis each time. There will be a reminder from the teacher each time. 'Number one leader, two lively, neat actions, please.' 'Change! New leader, work hard to make your shapes firm, clear and strong.' 'Change! New leader, where are you dancing. Always forwards? Or can you sometimes dance on the spot, turning even, or can you do a sideways travel somewhere?'

2 Each of the numbered teams performs by itself, behind the original leaders chosen by the teacher. Each is praised by the teacher and thanked with encouraging comments.

Lesson Plan 4 • 30 minutes
November

Theme: *Fireworks.*

Warm-up Activities
5 minutes

1 We started our last lesson with big, slow, bending and stretching movements on the spot. Can you now balance, tall and stretched on tiptoes, then run a few steps, jump up high, and show me another stretch in the air, keeping hands and feet together? Off you go!

2 Shoot your hands right up to the ceiling, like a rocket in space. Land softly with a nice 'give' in your knees and ankles.

3 Stand with feet and arms apart, high above your head – in the star shape that rockets make when they explode. Now, run a few steps and shoot straight up into another, beautifully wide star shape as you explode. Then land gently, squashing down carefully.

Movement Skills Training
15 minutes

1 Well done. I liked your straight and wide shapes in the air.

2 Before rockets 'Whoosh' into take-off, they have to be lit. Crouch low in a long, thin shape and pretend I have just lit your paper fuse. Show me your sizzling, starting actions.

3 Run into space for your take-off, 'Whoosh', and show me your explosion into a star shape, followed by your squashy landing.

4 From whooshing rockets, let's change to sparkling sparklers and hold one in each hand. Shake your hands quickly as you light up all the spaces around you, above, to sides, behind, high and low. Let your fingers shoot out and in quickly, like sparks flying.

5 Your hands can reach to different spaces at the same time or they can come together to make a double lot of sparks. Surprise me with your exciting, wandering spark makers.

6 From hands to feet now as you show me the actions of the little bangers that surprise us with their sudden, unexpected jumps. Jump quickly, sometimes on the spot, sometimes zigzagging. I will be listening for your sudden quick movement sounds, 'Bang! Bang! Bang!... Bang!... Bang!... Bang! Bang!' Go

Dance – Fireworks
10 minutes

1 What brilliant 'Bangs!' For our 'Fireworks' dance, choose which firework you want to be. Hands up... rockets... sparklers... bangers.

2 Sparklers go first, as you often do at firework parties, and keep going. Rockets, get ready.

3 Rockets, sizzle, whoosh and bang into star shapes, then drift slowly down. Keep repeating your performance. Bangers, get ready.

4 Lively, noisy bangers, off you go. Rockets and sparklers, keep going as well.

5 Rockets... stop. Sparklers... stop. Bangers... stop.

6 Join hands in groups of four. You can hold hands with the two people next to you in a circle, or all put your right hand in to make a star. As Catherine wheels, circle around slowly, once, with all groups moving clockwise. Then, do one complete circle, speeding up a little. Then slow down gradually for one circle, drop hands and scatter, sinking to the floor.

7 Well done. In our next practice, show me how your rocket, sparkler or banger moves in its own special way. As Catherine wheels, do one slow, one speeding up and one slowing down circle only.

Dance

Teaching notes and NC guidance
Development over 3 lessons

Pupils should be taught to adopt the best possible posture and use of the body. Through body movements in Dance we can express many things – moods, feelings and ideas. A firework display is the idea expressed here as we make the long, thin rocket's starting and flying shape, followed by its explosion into our biggest ever scattering body shape. The 'best possible posture and use of the body' is demonstrated through the starting shapes, actions and endings of each of the fireworks. Pupils are 'talking' to us through their body shapes and movements, often encouraged by the teacher's 'Show me your starting shape to tell me (express to me) which of the fireworks you are representing. Now show me the special ways of moving that we expect from a firework.' The focus is on the body's shape, size, tension, posture and use.

Warm-up Activities

1–3 The long, stretched arrow shape of the previous lesson is now held in a tall, still, balanced starting position before a run into an upwards jump with the whole body stretched. Imagining themselves as rockets, shooting upwards into space, and exploding outwards in a star shape, provides pupils with a real idea to inspire their actions. The highest, stretched jumps and gentle, squashy, controlled landings deserve to be shared with the rest of the class.

Movement Skills Training

1–3 Pupils' vocal 'Whoosh!' comes after a sizzling start to the rocket's fuse, and the short run, jump and explosion into the star shape. The hall should be an exciting mixture of rockets sizzling; taking off and flight; exploding into star shapes; and softly landing.

4–5 Both hands are used to make the sparklers light up all the spaces surrounding the dancers. Rapid fingers scattering, shooting in and out at speed, reach high, low, behind and out to the sides. In contrast with the very straight, accelerating, direct rocket flight, the sparklers shoot rapidly and unpredictably in every direction.

6 Equally unpredictably and suddenly, the little bangers jump from place to place across the floor accompanied by the sudden vocal sounds 'Bang!... Bang!... Bang! Bang!' of pupils.

Fireworks Dance

1–2 Volunteer sparklers start the dance, as is traditional at firework parties.

3 Sparklers keep going as rockets join in with their sizzling, whooshing, bang and scatter.

4 Noisy bangers, jumping about suddenly and unexpectedly, are the next group introduced by the teacher's accompanying commentary. The hall is filled with sparklers using huge spaces around the handlers; rockets taking off, exploding, drifting, and then starting all over again; and lively noisy bangers bouncing hither and thither about the floor space.

5 Each group of fireworks in turn is stopped by the teacher and each will hold the body shape that identifies them – the spiky-fingered sparklers; the scattered, fragmented rockets; and the tight, strong bangers.

6 All join hands in fours to represent Catherine wheels whose two circling actions and final scatter are chosen by the teacher to ensure a whole-class-together ending to the dance.

7 Whole dance is repeated to provide the class and the teacher with a special fireworks event.

Lesson Plan 5 • 30 minutes
December

Theme: *Christmas.*

Warm-up Activities
5 minutes

1 At Christmas time there is lots of travelling and meeting friends. Travel to the bouncy music, and visit every part of the room – sides, ends, corners as well as the middle. Go!

2 Keep travelling. When I sound the tambourine twice, meet, join up and dance with someone near you. You may say 'Hello!'

3 Keep together, travelling neatly. When I strike the tambourine once, dance by yourself. You may say 'Goodbye!'

4 Two beats on the tambourine means meet and join up with a partner, but not the same one again. 'Hello!' (Keep repeating.)

Movement Skills Training
15 minutes

1 In our last lesson our muscles worked to keep the rockets firm and strong. Pretend you have no muscles. You are all dangling bones. Show me your floppy travelling.

2 You should be feeling all floppy. Can you feel your arms, neck and shoulders joining the rattling, started by the legs moving?

3 On the spot, move your bones slowly to go from one floppy shape to another. Feel as if you are using no energy in your loose shapes. Pretend you are a skeleton, rattling from shape to shape.

4 Puppets move like you, rattling and loose. Sit and sag like a puppet. When I name a body part, pretend I am pulling a string attached to that part and lift it jerkily like a puppet. Left knee! Right elbow! Both shoulders! Whole body pulled by neck and shoulders! Slowly crumple down to your saggy starting position.

5 What kind of Christmas present puppet would you want to be – soldier, doll, clown, fairy, robot or dancer? Decide. Then start off, lying on the floor. Pretend someone is lifting you slowly with strings, then holding you just high enough to let you do your jerky, loose, puppet movements. Soldiers, dolls, clowns, fairies, robots, dancers or whatever, please rise and dance.

6 Stop in a shape that tells me what kind of puppet you have been, and slowly, jerkily, sag down to your starting position.

Dance – The Puppet Maker's Dream
10 minutes

1 The puppet maker is very sad. The puppets he (or she) has made for Christmas do not move properly. He cannot understand why.

2 The puppet maker walks up and down the lines of puppets on the shelves of the workshop. He stops often, lifts the imaginary strings of one or more puppets to bring them into action. The actions are poor, tired-looking and always too slow. The sad puppet maker moves on to a different group but they are just as poor. The sad puppet maker lies down, falls asleep and dreams.

3 Individuals, partners or small groups open their eyes, look keen and enthusiastic and rise up to sitting and standing position. With great style, they perform their distinctive, larger than life, floppy, loose dances, ending in a held shape before lowering back down to their sagging, limp positions on the floor.

4 The dancers become still. The puppet maker wakens, sits up and looks around him for the puppets with their excellent actions. All he sees are the same, poor, disappointing puppets.

Dance

Teaching notes and NC guidance
Development over 3 lessons

Pupils should be taught to:

a   **create simple characters and narratives.** The teacher's questioning focuses on the ways that pupils move to represent and express the puppets. 'Which body part is leading? Show me the slow lift and the opposite, quick flop. Show me, by your starting shape, which kind of puppet you want to be. What will be special about your soldier puppet's marching?'

b   **express feelings, moods and ideas.** The puppet maker will express his or her slowness, sadness, disappointment and tiredness through body movements associated with such moods and feelings – the bowed back and dragging feet; the drooping arm gestures and shoulder shrugging; the sagging, drooping whole body down to the lying, sleeping. The puppets will also express their characteristics through their movements – the swaggering soldier; the erratic clown; the neat and dainty fairy; the floppy doll; the stiff, almost jointless robots.

Warm-up Activities

1–4 Lively travelling, alone; joining with a partner to travel when the tambourine sounds twice; dancing alone when the tambourine sounds once; joining with a different partner when the tambourine sounds twice, is a great favourite with all primary school age groups. Being allowed to give a 'Hello!' welcome to each new partner is an extra attraction.

Movement Skills Training

1–4 Applying different degrees of body tension is a way of enhancing a performance and adding variety and quality to movements. In contrast with the firm, strong rockets of the last lesson, the floppy, limp, saggy body movements express the true nature of puppets. Much direct teaching is used to develop the floppy, dangling feeling as they travel, move on the spot or sit. The use of imagery and imagination – 'Pretend you are a skeleton, rattling from shape to shape' – helps the class to feel and create the movements they want to express.

5–6 Being asked to plan to represent the identity of a character through body movements is a big challenge to the class. They should also try to express something of the personality of their chosen puppet through different body shapes and tensions used.

The Puppet Maker's Dream Dance

1–2 Movements, previously of puppets, are used to express the movements of the sad puppet maker whose Christmas puppets are a failure. One of the class can represent the puppet maker sadly inspecting groups of the rest of the class as unsatisfactory puppets. Tired, and without hope, the puppet maker lies down, falls asleep and dreams.

3   Within the dream, the six groups of puppets in the class come alive, expressing the keenness, enthusiasm, poise and style that has been missing in the toyshop. Using appropriate shapes and different levels of effort and degrees of body tension, the proud erect soldier, erratic clown, limp rag doll, dancing, pirouetting fairy, angular, stiff robot and loose-limbed dancing puppet are all made to be different individuals who end their dream dance in a body shape of their style, before lowering back to their poor, sagging floor positions.

4   The puppet maker wakens. In vain, he or she looks for the excellence seen in the dream.

Lesson Plan 6 • 30 minutes
January

Theme: *Winter.*

Warm-up Activities
5 minutes

January is often the coldest month. Let's pretend we are coming to school and moving to keep warm. Please join in the singing:

This is the way we rub and run, (fast little steps and quick rubbing of chest, upper arms, shoulders)
rub and run, rub and run,
this is the way we rub and run on a cold and frosty morning.

This is the way we walk and shake, (quick, lively, big shakes of legs and arms)
walk and shake, walk and shake,
this is the way we walk and shake on a cold and frosty morning.

Repeat, then invite suggestions for other actions from the class. For example, hug and skip; shake and bounce; bend and stretch.

Movement Skills Training
15 minutes

1   Each of my two cards has three winter words for you to think about, before deciding which set of words to choose.
    Card 1 (Stream)   RUSH   FREEZE   SKATE
    Card 2 (Snow)   FLOAT   DRIFT   MELT

2   What kind of movement does the rushing stream make you think of? Bubbling and splashing; hurrying and spreading; sometimes crashing over stones. Show me your rushing.

3   Will the 'Freeze' be sudden or gradual? Gradual, becoming smoother, steadier, firmer, still, hard, jagged. Rush for three or four seconds, then start your freezing. Go!

4   Well done, frozen streams. Skating can be performed expertly with never a stumble, or inexpertly with lots of wobbly arm waving. Brilliant or wobbly... off you go!

5   Snowflakes now. Can you tell me how they float down? Lightly; gently fluttering; then softly landing. Show me how you might slowly float, going from space to space, before coming to rest.

6   Those were excellent, gentle, snowflake movements. Well done. If your snowflake is suddenly struck by a strong wind, how will it respond and drift? High and low; with changes of direction; with pauses between gusts; with sudden, fast movements; all before settling, still in a snowflake shape. Ready for the wind? Drift!

7   When the snow melts into a puddle on the ground, it will be a slow and smooth movement, spreading outwards. Start in your snowflake shape, with parts of your body off the floor. Now melt slowly.

Dance — Winter Words
10 minutes

1   Hands up the 'stream' group. Hands up the 'snowflakes' group.

2   Show me your starting shape, which should tell me if you are going to rush or float – two very different actions.

3   I will call out the pairs of words to guide your timing. Rush or float... freeze or drift... skate or melt...

4   Hold your final position, please, with the skaters in a clever or awkward position and shape.

Dance

Teaching notes and NC guidance
Development over 3 lessons

Pupils should:

a **be involved in the continuous process of planning, performing and evaluating.** This is an excellent opportunity for planning because the performance of the three actions is short, and for performing because there is ample time for practising, repeating and remembering the little sequence. Pupils can then reflect on the performance by the other half of the class. Helpful suggestions are invited to bring about an improvement. Such observations by pupils are valuable because the teacher is not always able to see everything. Performances are enhanced as pupils try hard to be selected for praise.

b **compose and control their movements by varying shape, size, direction, speed and tension.** Speed and tension contrasts are evident in the rushing of the stream and the gentle floating of the snowflake. The hard, jagged frozen water shapes contrast with the loose, spreading snowflakes. The high and low level and direction changes of the snowflakes in flight can be matched by the erratic skating of an inexpert skater. Awareness of the elements of movement quality, variety and contrast are able to be taught and experienced in this lesson.

Warm-up Activities

1 The 'On a cold and frosty morning' action song is well known and popular in primary schools, and is an excellent, instant start to a January lesson. The teacher-leader sings and moves and the class copy, quickly picking up the repeated actions and the words. Other ideas include 'This is the way we skip to school; dance in the hall; chase outside.'

Movement Skills Training

1 The two cards each have three seasonal action words to consider before choosing one.

2–4 The teaching is almost totally a series of challenging questions to make the class think about the nature of the actions and then try them out. 'What kind of movement ...?' 'Show me....' 'Is freezing sudden or smooth?' 'Will you be a brilliant or a wobbly skater?' are all questions designed to make the class think ahead to 'see' an intended outcome.

5–7 Helped again by the teacher's questioning, the class consider and practise three contrasting types of snowfall movements – the gentle, light floating; the faster drifting in gusts of strong wind; and the settling, melting into a puddle on the ground. The whole class is taught to consider and feel both the stream's and the snow's movements before deciding which is their favourite for the dance climax of the lesson.

Winter Words Dance

1–2 The whole class is invited to choose to dance to express their choice of stream or snow winter actions. Their choice is obvious from their starting body shapes. Holding a 'rush' body shape with its firm, balanced readiness for quick dashes is very different from holding a gentle, light, 'float' shape prior to weightless floating and hovering. This initial request for good shape and body tension emphasises the importance of these elements throughout.

3–4 To avoid over-long repetitions of actions by pupils, the teacher calls out the pairs of words giving each enough time. The dance ends with a held shape by skaters and the melted, spread out snow. Groups then perform for the other group to observe and comment on.

Lesson Plan 7 • 30 minutes
January/February

Theme: *Traditional, folk-dance style creative dance.*

Warm-up Activities
5 minutes

1   Dance on the spot for eight counts, then travel through good spaces for the next eight counts.

2   'On the spot' can include skipping, setting or bouncing in time with the music. Let your travelling really go somewhere as a good contrast. On the spot, 3, 4, 5, 6, 7, now travel; 1, 2, travelling well, 5, 6, now on the spot.

3   Find a partner. One of you show your dancing on the spot to the other and both remember it. Then the other partner shows their travelling for both to practise and remember.

4   Decide whether to dance side by side, or following the leader as you perform your shared choice.

Teach One-couple Figures to be Linked Creatively
15 minutes

Partner on the left as couple face top of set is A. Partner on the right is B. Each figure takes eight bars of the music

1   Dance around partner and back. A dances around the front of B and back to place, four counts. B repeats around A, dancing for four counts.

2   Cast off on own side (A turns to left, B turns to right) and dance to bottom for four counts. Turn in, join hands to dance to top and back to own places.

3   Change places with partner, four counts, giving right hands, then four to change back to own places, giving left hands.

4   Dance down middle of set, four counts, with hands joined, turn and dance back to top and own places, four counts.

5   Back to back or Do-si-do. Both go forwards, passing right shoulders, and back, passing left shoulders, without turning body around, i.e. keep facing partner's side of dance. Four counts each way.

Couples Plan and Practise own 32-bar Dance
10 minutes

Music: Any 32-bar, English or Scottish country dance.

Formation: Sets of one couple.

Each person can select two of the five figures above that he or she wishes to include in their four-figure dance. Both partners share in deciding the order of the figures to ensure a neat, smooth flow from figure to figure; variety in direction and in being joined or separate; and an ending that appeals to both.

Dance

Teaching notes and NC guidance
Development over 3 lessons

Pupils should be taught to:

a **respond to music.** With beginners we use slightly quicker music, and they can be asked to 'Stand still and clap your hands in time with this folk-dance music' before going into their warm-up activities. The music is phrased in groups of eight bars and the teacher's rhythmic accompaniment and chanting of the actions helps the class to 'feel' the music and to keep with it. 'On the spot, lively movements, 5, 6, now you travel; travel, travel; lively travel, 5, 6, on the spot.' Taking exactly eight bars for each figure of the dance is most important, so that pupils arrive back and go straight into the next figure without marking time if early, or dash in, in poor style, if late. The teacher can keep them with the music by accompanying each figure. 'Cast off, own side, 3, meet and turn; up the middle, hands joined, back to starting places.'

b **perform a number of dances from different times and places.** Including some traditional dances of the British Isles. In this easy introduction to folk dance the pupils are learning actual steps and figures from English and Scottish dances, and their own created dances are folk dances in style and pattern.

Warm-up Activities

1–2 During the eight-count action on the spot, pupils should be looking for a good space to dance through for the travelling eight steps. Simple skipping, on the spot and travelling, will suffice for the whole dance and can be encouraged and improved for this lesson.

3–4 Partner A shows his or her own dancing on the spot and partner B shows his or her travelling. Both then combine to perform their shared dance. Partners can be one behind the other for the travelling, or with one or both hands joined, elbows linked, or hand on shoulder.

Teach One-couple Figures to be Linked Creatively

1 Teacher and a partner can demonstrate each figure once, slowly without music, emphasising 'Use the correct number of counts each time for the figure, never arriving early or late.' The teacher's chanting helps this. 'Around for 2, back to places, 3, 4. Partners dance around, back to places, 3, 4.'

2 The cast off on own side, turning in, joining hands to dance back to top to own places needs a good demonstration to show how to be back in own places after joining and coming up the middle of the set. 'Cast off, 2, 3, hands joined; up the middle, 2, part to own places.'

3 In the right and left hands changing of places across the set, partners look back at each other as they help each other back to own places.

4 Down the middle of the set and back again happens often and partners need to be told 'Down the middle, 3, turn to face the top; up the middle, 3, back to own places.'

5 In 'Do-si-do', often danced in English country dancing, each pupil keeps facing forwards towards partner's side of the set. 'Forwards for 2, passing right shoulders; back for 2, passing left shoulders' gives lots of time to do the figure.

Couples Plan and Practise Own 32-Bar Dance

Each couple chooses two of the five figures and they share in deciding the varied, flowing order to a favourite ending.

Lesson Plan 8 • 30 minutes
February

Theme: *Traditional folk dance.*

Warm-up Activities
5 minutes

1 Skip by yourself, visiting every part of the room.

2 If the floor is suddenly crowded, keep skipping on the spot, then travel on when there is plenty of room.

3 Skip for eight counts, then join hands with someone and dance for eight counts. After these eight counts, separate and dance by yourself for eight counts. Then take a different partner for the next eight counts.

4 By yourself, 3, 4, 5, 6, join a partner. Hands joined, 3, 4, 5, 6, 7, split up. By yourself, 3, 4, 5, 6, find a new partner. Dance together, 3, 4, 5, 6, now split up. On your own, 3, 4, 5, 6, 7, 8.

Teach Figures of New Dance — Cumberland Reel
15 minutes

Formation: Longways set of two couples.

1 Couples form right- and left-hand star. Right hand to dancer diagonally opposite and wheel around for four counts. Left hand to dancer diagonally opposite and dance back to starting places. On the left-hand wheel, break the star on count three to let you finish in your own places on count four.

2 First couple dance down the centre and back to their place. Assist each other with your right hands. Going down, turn on count four to give you time to return to top of set on count three, to be in your own places on count four.

3 Both couples face top of set for casting to left and right. A casts to the left, B casts to the right. Second couple follow. First couple make an arch at the bottom, the second couple go under and promenade to top of set, hands joined. First couple follow.

4 All promenade around to the left with the second couple leading, back to set formation where the new first couple can start.

Dance — Cumberland Reel
10 minutes

Music: *Cumberland Reel* by Blue Mountain Band (EFDS), from Community Dances Manual 1, or any 32-bar dance.

Formation: Longways set of four, five or six couples.

Bars 1–8 Two top couples right and left hand star.

Bars 9–16 First couple dance down the centre and back.

Bars 17–24 A casts left and B casts right, others following. First couple make an arch at the bottom, others go under the arch and promenade up the centre to top of set.

Bars 25–32 All promenade around to the left, followed by first couple.

Repeat with new first and second couples doing the right and left hand star.

Dance

Teaching notes and NC guidance
Development over 3 lessons

Pupils should be taught to:

perform a number of dances from different times and places, including some traditional dances of the British Isles. Because the dance involves two-couples only, it is taught in two couple sets to use the whole class. Within this formation, each of the couples has a turn at being first couple – that is, the couple nearer the top of the set – and a turn at being second couple. In the long set of four or more couples, each first couple leads the dance once only, and then finishes in bottom place while a new first couple re-starts the dance. This is an easy dance with both Scottish and English versions.

Pupils should demonstrate that they can:

a work safely as members of a team. Working sensibly, safely and co-operatively; being in the right place at the right time; not pushing and shoving others; and trying to dance neatly in time with the music, are all essential elements of an enjoyable and successful folk dance lesson.

b repeat sequences with increasing control and accuracy. The ability to remember and repeat a series or sequence of linked actions or movements is a prime National Curriculum requirement. This dance, with its four-part repeating pattern, gives excellent practice in the thinking ahead required for a successful performance. The teacher will ensure that there is a special focus during each practice to ensure improvement.

Warm-up Activities

1–2 Pupils are trained to avoid crowded areas and to look for good spaces. There will be times, however, when an area becomes unexpectedly busy, and it is necessary to inform the class what to do then. Many would not think of dancing on the spot, waiting for a good space to return.

3–4 Dancing by yourself for eight counts, alternating with dancing with a partner for eight, will start with the teacher's counting to eight to help pupils feel the phrases of eight steps. If this is well practised, the class should be able to count the groups of eight and then do the changes without always needing a teacher reminder.

Teach Figures of New Dance

1 In the right- and left-hand star or wheel, the pairs of joined hands will be held at the height of the shortest dancer for his or her comfort, with emphasis on 'Back in own places on four.'

2 'Down the middle and up' is often used in English and Scottish country dance, remembering to be back in own places, standing ready for next figure, after the 'back for four'.

3 The 'cast off to own sides' starts with dancers all facing to top of set, before peeling off to go down the outside of their side of the set. Emphasise 'To top of set, 2, 3, into own places.'

4 A cross-wrists grip is used in the 'Promenade left, 2, 3, turn; up, 2, 3, into own places'.

Dance – Cumberland Reel

Sets are told that the couples nearest to the music, often at the platform end, are the first couples who, in this dance, have one turn only at being the first couple. After making the arch, the original first couple stay at the bottom of the set. Two new first and second couples start the dance again with the right- and left-hand star or wheel. All should be watching and thinking ahead.

Lesson Plan 9 • 30 minutes
March

Theme: *Body contact sounds and rhythms.*

Warm-up Activities
5 minutes

1   In our last lesson we danced in time with folk dance music. Let's travel to some folk dance music and feel the sets of eight counts. By yourselves... go!

2   Can you include some kind of change for each set of eight counts? Travel; dance on the spot; change the action; or change direction.

3   This time, ignore one set of eight beats and stand still. Then join in again, exactly in time with the music, eight bars later. At any one time, some of you will be standing, quietly counting up to eight, while all the others are travelling around. Go!

Movement Skills Training
15 minutes

1   Sit down and listen to the nursery rhyme I am sounding with my hands and feet. Please do not shout out if you know which one it is. Listen, and then put your hand up to tell me.

2   'Jack and Jill went up the hill' is sounded with hands on the floor. 'To fetch a pail of water' is sounded with feet beating on the floor. 'Jack fell down and broke his crown' is sounded with cupped hands on opposite shoulders, arms crossed. 'And Jill came tumbling after' uses hands and feet on the floor.

3   After identifying the nursery rhyme, the pupils remain seated, say the words and accompany the teacher in sounding them out on floor, hands and shoulders.

4   Stand and sing out the first line, making a rhythmic clapping of hands. You can walk forwards, rising up on tiptoes. 'Jack and Jill went up the hill'.

5   Sound feet strongly on the spot. 'To fetch a pail of water'.

6   On 'Jack fell down and broke his crown', clap hands, starting high and coming down (like Jack) with a huge clap on crown.

7   'And Jill came tumbling after', skipping with crossed-arm handclaps from shoulders down to a final slap on thighs.

8   Well done. Let's practise again with every word accompanied by a hand or foot movement, sounding clearly. Sing, clap, dance... go!

Dance — Jack and Jill
10 minutes

1   Find a partner and decide who is one and who is two.

2   On line one of the rhyme, one stays on the spot, making feet and hand sounds. Number two circles around one, with lively feet beating the floor and hands slapping sides or thighs. 'Jack and Jill went up the hill.'

3   On line two, change over and repeat, as for line one. 'To fetch a pail of water'.

4   On line three, partners face each other, with hands high, do small galloping steps to same side, and clap, bringing hands low for a loud clap on crown. 'Jack fell down and broke his crown.'

5   'And Jill came tumbling after'. Partners, still face each other, clap own hands twice, (and Jill); clap own knees, (came tumbling); then clap each other's hands at head height (after).

6   Development. Partners can create their own short, body rhythms dance to a different nursery rhyme. Pairs demonstrate and others try to identify the new nursery rhyme.

Dance

Teaching notes and NC guidance
Development over 3 lessons

Pupils should be taught to:

a **try hard to consolidate their performances** and gain a sense of achievement. Performances will only be improved and consolidated if the teacher works hard at demanding neat, controlled actions, provides ample opportunities for practice, looks out for and comments on good quality work, and uses demonstrations to identify the main features being pursued.

b **respond to a range of stimuli, through dance.** In the same way that a Dance lesson should include variety and contrast for maximum interest, a Dance programme should include many kinds of inspiration to make the series of lessons interesting, relevant, seasonal, challenging, surprising and exciting. In addition to music, which is widely used, sound as a stimulus can be provided by percussion instruments; the chanting of the rhythm of words, phrases, names, place names, numbers, food; action songs and rhymes; and by body contact sounds with nursery rhymes, as here. Varied stimuli also include: actions; flash cards; objects; moods and feelings; nature; stories; seasonal events and festivals; work actions; pictures; outings; animals; numbers; work going on in class; and things of particular interest to teacher and class.

Warm-up Activities

1 Clapping in time with the eight-bar phrasing of the music is a good idea, immediately before pupils travel in time with the music. The skipping rhythm of most folk-dance music is perfect for the typical speed of primary school skipping/travelling. The teacher will chant 'skip, 2, 3, 4, 5, 6, 7 and 8.'

2 The teacher's chanting will now include a reminder of the challenge. 'Skip, 2, 3, 4, 5, 6, new action, please!'

3 Gradually, the teacher will chant less and less, making the class count out their own sets of eight. 'Skip, 2, 3, 4, 5, 6, now you change! Still, 2, 3, 4, 5, 6, now you count, please!'

Movement Skills Training

1 'Listen to the nursery rhyme. Do not call out if you know it' is an important start.

2 Four different body parts sounds – hands, feet, hands on shoulders, and hands and feet – are used and usually the nursery rhyme will be recognised and named by several pupils.

3 Teacher and class, seated, sound out and say the words together.

4–7 The teacher demonstrates each line's action and method of sound making, and repeats the line and the action along with the class.

8 By saying each word slowly, it is possible to accompany each word with the soundings of hands and feet – walking and singing; sounding feet on the spot; clapping hands and clap on crown; and hand-claps from shoulders down to thighs.

Jack and Jill Dance

1–5 The teacher, with a partner, demonstrates the whole dance, slowly. Then partners say and perform one line at a time, reminded each time by the teacher of what is coming next. After several successful line-by-line practices, the class dance the whole dance through.

Lesson Plan 10 • 30 minutes
March/April

Theme: *Circus.*

Music: TV Sport from *Festival of Music* by Central Band of the R.A.F.

Warm-up Activities
6 minutes

1 For our parade into town, march anti-clockwise in a big circle. Wave to the towns-people. 'Hello! We're back. Come and see us.'

2 Join hands in a big circle. From a low starting position, travel forwards to a medium height, tent shape, then back to your circle. On your second go, travel forwards and make a high tent shape on tiptoes

3 Trapezists: Space out in one half of the room, facing the other half of the class. With high, stretched arms, travel forwards, swinging to a high level. Swing back to a lower level. Repeat.

4 Tightrope walkers: Each half of the class faces a different side of the room. Hold your arms sideways for your wobbly balance. Balance step forwards, forwards, wobble, wobble; balance step back, back, wobble, wobble. Repeat.

Movement Skills Training
12 minutes

1 In our groups of four, decide which circus actions you will make into a pattern you can remember and repeat. Will you be clowns, jugglers, trapezists, acrobats, tightrope walkers, strong-men or -women, or will you be the band?

2 Let your actions show the main feature of the circus people. For example, the strong-man or -woman pulling the imaginary rope dragging the others along, expresses 'Pull them hard, pull them strong, look at my muscles, look at my muscles (flexing biceps).'

3 Clowns might do a funny walk on heels, spin around with one leg high, fall down slowly, bounce up quickly, and keep repeating it.

4 Tightrope walkers and trapezists can use the sequence we did earlier in the lesson or bring in your own ideas.

5 Jugglers, you can juggle in front, in front; overhead, overhead; up the back, up the back.

6 Whatever you decide, remember to make a short, three- or four-part pattern that you can repeat. While you are practising it, one of you may say the actions to remind your group.

Dance – Circus
12 minutes

1 Parade, anti-clockwise, around in a big circle.

2 Hands should be joined in the circle to make the big top.

3 Members of class at opposite ends of the room face each other as they trapeze forwards and backwards, twice.

4 Members of class facing opposite sides of the room perform the wobbly tightrope walker's balance-walk forwards and backwards.

5 In groups of four, perform own circus actions.

6 Lowering of big top. All hands joined in a circle, high on tiptoes, in a high tent shape. All travel back, hands still joined, lowering down and back. Then all travel forwards to a medium height, half-lowered tent shape, then travel all the way back, lowering tent right down to floor.

7 Parade out of town. Transfer from lowered tent, circle shape, to the big circle, leaving town, clockwise, waving 'Goodbye. We'll see you next year.'

Dance

Teaching notes and NC guidance
Development over 4 lessons

Pupils should be taught to:

create simple characters and narratives. The expression of the identity of the characters being created is done through our bodily movements. We are not miming, acting or contorting our facial muscles. Our whole body is being used to represent the style of movement we associate with the characters. Their typical actions, shapes, amount of effort used and any particular idiosyncrasies are all included in the movement expression.

Pupils should be able to show that they can:

a   respond imaginatively to the various challenges. The start and finish of this dance are teacher-directed. The middle of the dance involves the groups of four deciding which of the work actions they want to perform, and then planning to incorporate those actions into an easily remembered repeating pattern.

b   repeat sequences with increasing control and accuracy. Each group of four is helped and encouraged to plan its repeating pattern of actions to provide interest, variety and contrast. The sequence is short enough to be easily remembered and repeated and long enough to give a good expression of the characters, as in the teacher-led, tightrope walkers' sequence in the warm-up.

Warm-up Activities

1   Teacher and class stand in a circle, all facing anti-clockwise. When the music starts, they walk around, in step with the marching music, waving to advertise their arrival in town.

2   All join hands, facing the centre, to travel forwards and back, twice, to make the tent shape.

3   Trapezists, all well spaced out behind teacher-demonstrator, swing forwards and back, twice.

4   Tight-rope walkers all face another direction, still behind teacher-demonstrator, for 'Step forwards, forwards, wobble, wobble, wobble; step back, back, wobble, wobble, wobble.'

Movement Skills Training

1   It helps pupil decision-making if the teacher has a card showing lots of work actions. If pupils' deciding is too time-consuming, the teacher can ensure a good mix by telling each group what to practise. Each quartet is given its place, widely spaced apart from other groups because there will be six or seven groups, some of whom need lots of space as in swinging/trapezing.

2   Groups are asked to show the one main feature of their work action, and to try to plan and remember a repeating sequence. 'Oompah, oompah, hit the drum' as they walk, as a band, behind a leader, playing both trombone and drum with big arm flourishes, for example.

3-4   Clowns are given help with a teacher demonstration; tight-rope walkers and trapezists repeat and improve actions already practised with the emphasis on 'Big actions so that spectators at the back of the tent can see what you are doing.'

5   Juggling is often chosen and needs good use of space, around, behind and above you.

6   Planning a three- or four-parter is a big challenge, calling for originality, variety and enthusiasm.

Circus Dance

1-7   For the first practice with the music, the teacher reminds and joins in with the class all the way to 'Go to your places for your own work actions' when the music is paused and the class stand, ready. With the teacher's accompanying commentary, the dance is continued to the end. In the second practice, they dance all the way through, non-stop, to the music.

Lesson Plan 11 • 30 minutes
May

Theme: *Traditional folk dance.*

Warm-up Activities
5 minutes

1 Partners, decide who is one and who is two. Travel, side by side, with number one deciding what to do and where to do it. Change the action after each set of eight bars of music. A change of direction, also on eight, always looks attractive.

2 Number two, can you decide on actions to take you apart, and then bring you together again, allowing eight counts for each?

3 Partners, practise a four-part, repeating A: B: B: A pattern of travelling together; parting, closing; parting, closing; and travelling together.

Teach a Dance — Djatchko Kolo (Yugoslavian Folk Dance)
20 minutes

Music: Djatchko Kolo, Society for International Folk Dancing (cassette and book 3)

Formation: Open circle with teacher at the right hand open end. This simple dance can be learned easily with the teacher calling out and demonstrating each movement straightaway with the music, with the class copying the teacher.

Figure 1

Bar 1	Beat 1	Step right foot to right.
	2	Close left foot to right foot.
	3	Step right foot to right.
	4	Swing left foot across right foot.
Bar 2	Beats 1–4	Repeat bar 1 to the left, starting with left foot.
Bars 3 & 4		Repeat all of above.

Figure 2

Bar 5	Beat 1	Step right foot to right.
	2	Swing left foot across right foot.
	3	Step left foot to left.
	4	Swing right foot across left foot.
Bar 6	Beats 1–4	Repeat bar 5.

Figure 3

Bars 7 & 8	Starting with right foot, perform seven little walking steps to the right and point heel of right foot on floor on the last beat of bar 8.
Bars 9 & 10	Seven steps to left and point heel of left foot on the floor, on the last beat of bar 10.

Keep repeating the dance from the beginning.

Revise a Favourite Dance
5 minutes

This can be a folk dance such as the 'Cumberland Reel' or, for variety, a creative dance such as 'Circus' of the previous month.

Dance

Teacher notes and NC Guidance Development over 3 Lessons

Pupils should be taught to:

a **be physically active.** The challenge for the teacher is to 'get on with it' by keeping explanations clear and short; by being confident that the class can keep up with him or her in going through this easy dance; and by rhythmically accompanying the actions while dancing with the pupils in the circle. 'Step to right, close, step right, swing left; step to left, close, step left, swing right.' Hearing the instructions and following the teacher's lead make this an easy dance to learn, with few stoppages.

b **perform a number of dances from different times and places.** With younger, less experienced dancers, teaching in a circle where all can see and be seen by the teacher is the easiest way. A dance from the 'different times and places' repertoire will ideally be something to which interested members of staff might contribute. Many teachers will have no experience of folk dance from their schooldays or college training.

Pupils should be able to show that they can remember and repeat a series of movements performed previously. Because this is such a simple dance, there should be ample time to include a favourite dance with which to finish the lesson. The class can be asked 'What dance shall we finish with?' to let the teacher see which are their particular favourites, or the teacher can decide to include a dance because it provides a good contrast with the one just learned.

Warm-up Activities

1 Lead partner, number one, is challenged to plan a series of eight-count travel actions, always ensuring, as a good leader, to take partner and self into good spaces for these travels.

2 New lead partner, number two, has the more difficult challenge of parting and closing actions – chasse sideways; step to side, close feet, step, close; skipping, almost on the spot, with little travel to sides; marching, bouncing or skipping, etc.

3 With both pupils contributing, this is a real partner creation and there should be demonstrations by hard-working, creative, enthusiastic couples to recognise and appreciate them and to share and learn from their brilliant ideas.

Teach a Dance – Djatchko Kolo

Figure 1
The music, at the start, is very slow, making it easy for the class to watch and copy the steps led by the teacher. The simple 'Step, close up, step, swing' going to the circle's right is then repeated to the left. Holding hands in the circle also helps to lead any confused dancers in the right direction.

Figure 2
The 'Step right, swing right, step left, swing left' is also repeated and can be done simply standing on the supporting foot as you swing the other, or you can do a little bounce up on the swing.

Figure 3
All in the circle, walk-step anti-clockwise for seven counts with a firm heel press to the floor on count 8. This circle travel and heel press is repeated to the left. This easy dance is then repeated several times for the beginning, ideally with less teacher reminders each time.

Lesson Plan 12 • 30 minutes
June

Theme: *Fast and slow.*

Warm-up Activities
5 minutes

1 Can you be very clever and show me a leg action on the spot; then a short travel; then big body movements, such as bending, stretching, twisting, rising or lowering, on the spot?

2 Show me your starting position for your first action, with arms, legs and body nicely balanced and ready. Begin!

3 Stop! Now look for a good space for your short travelling action. I hope it's different from the first action. Ready? Go!

4 Stop! On the spot, show me your one or two whole body movements.

5 Stop in a held shape. Well done. Keep practising all three actions again in your own time. Show me your still shape at the start and finish, each time. Off you go!

Movement Skills Training
10 minutes

1 Stand ready, again, for your first leg action on the spot. Pretend the floor is hot and do the action as fast as you can. Go!

2 Stop! Now, do your travelling action at equally high speed to take you to a space. Make every part of your body join in.

3 On the spot, find a good balance position for your high-speed body movements – up and down, in and out, around and back, go!

4 Wow! You looked like out-of-control machines. Well done. Now, like machines with almost no power, do your three actions in ultra-slow motion, just moving and no more. Slow-mo... go!

5 Use your joints fully to make your slow motion a whole body slow motion. Don't cut down on the size of your actions. Once again, v-e-e-r-y slo-o-ow-ly, begin!

Dance — Fast Forwards, Fast Back, Slow-Motion Replay
15 minutes

1 Find a partner. I want you both to think about a favourite TV sport that you might like to perform in an unusual dance.

2 Performers, show me by your starting shape what your sport is. I see swimmers, cricketers, golfers, footballers, tennis and netball players, athletes, jockeys, skiers, canoeists, gliders, hockey and rugby players, and weight lifters. What brilliant variety.

3 Off you go. Practise your chosen sport and see if you can make a little repeating pattern of three or four parts that's easy to remember (e.g. forehand, backhand, run in and smash; or jump, catch, run in and score; or swing, swing, hit the golf ball).

4 One of you stand ready to perform. Partner, sit down. Pretend you are about to watch sport on TV. As you press the control buttons, say 'normal' or 'fast forwards' or 'fast back' or 'slow motion', and your sporty partner must immediately respond. Be sensible, please, and don't use 'fast back' or 'fast forwards' for more than a few seconds. Over to you, operators. Begin.

5 Stop! Sportspersons, sit down beside your operators and tell them what you thought of their button pushing. How would you like them to change to help you perform better?

6 Same dancers and operators. One more improved practice, please.

7 Well done, dancers and operators. That looked much better. Now, change duties and we'll do the whole thing again twice.

8 Half of the class can now enjoy watching the other half.

Dance

Teaching notes and NC guidance
Development over 4 lessons

Pupils should be taught to:

a **respond to a range of stimuli through Dance.** The remote control for their television and the many sporting events on TV are well-known, relevant stimuli for most modern youngsters. Paradoxically, these stimuli in real life can destroy regular pupil participation in sport.

b **respond imaginatively to the various challenges.** The pupils are given responsibility for deciding their sport and planning the actions to be represented. Responses will be original, and, with teacher encouragement, might become imaginative.

Pupils should be able to show that they can make simple judgements about their own and others' performances. It is important to provide opportunities for observing demonstrations when pupils have worked so hard at planning and practising something original. Encouraging, friendly comments give pleasure to performers and inspire them to further improvement. Comments made often have relevance for others.

Warm-up Activities

1 The big leg action on the spot; short travel; big body movements on the spot, repeating, a: b: c, three-part sequence, is a lively and varied start to the lesson.

2 The big leg action on the spot will probably use other big body parts vigorously and the still, balanced, whole body action and shape starting position will give a preview.

3 A different travel action is needed with the challenge 'Make it a short travel action.' In other words, we do not want a long run and jump.

4 One or two 'whole body movements' on the spot should ideally feel joints in arms, spine and neck, shoulders, hips, waist and legs moving to their fullest bend and stretch.

5 The requested 'Still shape start and finish', with the three actions in between linked together smoothly, neatly and with control, will be a constant part of the pursuit of quality work.

Movement Skills Training

1–2 The use of imagery is intended to help communicate what it is that we are trying to express. 'Imagine that the floor is hot... Imagine you are looking for a cooler floor space.'

3–5 The whole body movements, practised earlier, are now done at high speed and then in slow motion. 'Use your joints fully' and 'Don't cut down on the size of your actions' should fill the room with massive bendings, stretchings, twistings, turnings and arm bendings and stretchings in every direction. Ultra-slow, ultra-big whole body movements are not often requested and need to be experienced and practised for a successful performed dance climax.

Fast Forward, Fast Back, Slow-Motion Replay Dance

1–3 As in the 'Circus Dance' it helps the class if the teacher holds up a list of typical sports that the class might like to consider for their dance, which might have been called 'TV Sport'. Emphasise 'Practise on the spot, inside a pretend TV set. Make a three- or four-part repeating sequence that you can remember. Fast forward and back are hard. Use seldom.'

4–8 Sportspersons and operators each perform; receive advice from partner; perform after being helped; and then all demonstrate in a half-watch-half, observe and comment dance climax.

Lesson Plan 13 • 30 minutes
July

Theme: *Feelings.*

Warm-up Activities
5 minutes

I am sure that you will include 'Happy' among your end of school year feelings as we come to the summer holidays. Please join me in singing the words as we do our lively skipping, marching or bouncing around:

If you're happy and you know it, clap your hands,
If you're happy and you know it, clap your hands,
If you're happy and you know it, and you really want
*   to show it,*
If you're happy and you know it, clap your hands

If you're happy and you know it, swagger around,
*   wave to friends, punch the air, bounce and*
*   bounce, etc.*

Movement Skills Training
15 minutes

1   Find a partner and sit down, together, with one piece of percussion to be used later. I want you to agree on three action words that might describe your first year in junior school. Word one might be a shy, quiet, unsure start, creeping or gliding on to your little stage. Word two will be more lively, self-confident, growing, stretching, spreading or gesturing. Word three, for the end of the year, might be any of the happy actions we have practised, or it might be quite a sad closing in on yourself or waving 'Goodbye' as you fade away.

2   Choose your three action words. Number one, practise first with your partner watching carefully, ready to make a helpful suggestion for improvement. Let each action have a still start and finish position with a good body shape showing it off.

3   Sit down, number one, and listen to your partner's friendly advice. It might be about the action, shape, speed or timing. Having been helped, number one, perform again please.

4   Now change places to let number two practise the same three action words. Let your body movements tell us about your feelings and use your whole body as you do it.

5   Number two, sit down beside your partner to be given some friendly, helpful advice to improve your performance.

6   Number two, perform again and try to use the advice given.

Dance — Feelings
10 minutes

1   Number one, stand ready to perform your three actions. Number two, use the percussion quietly to accompany your partner. Start and stop the sound to make each action have a still start and finish position. Percussionist, take charge. Begin.

2   Well done. One more practice with the same dancer. Try your best.

3   Change places, please, and start when you are both ready. Practise twice and remember to separate the three actions.

4   Pairs will watch pairs now. Observers, try to guess what the three actions are. Each partner has a turn at performing.

5   You have all seen a couple performing and suggested what the three actions were. Let's look at several couples chosen for their interesting, excellent, clear and expressive performances.

Dance

Teaching notes and NC guidance
Development over 3 lessons

Pupils should be taught to:

express feelings, moods and ideas. The lesson might have been introduced by the teacher explaining 'In this month's lesson we are trying to express feelings and emotions by the way we move. We must only do this by the way we move.' The physical expressions of happiness in the warm-up with the hand-clapping, swaggering and waving and so on, all focus on the whole body and the way it is moving.

Pupils should be able to show that they can:

a **respond imaginatively to** the various challenges. The challenges are 'shared choice'. The teacher suggests the nature of the three actions but the pupils decide on the exact responses and words and have ample opportunities to plan and perform imaginatively.

b **repeat sequences with increasing control and accuracy.** When the performance is as short as here, it is easy to repeat, adapt, practise, improve and remember one's sequence.

c **make simple judgements effectively** to improve the accuracy, quality and variety of their own performance. Partner work provides the best opportunity for someone to look at what you are doing, to comment on it, and to help you improve.

Warm-up Activities

It is hoped that smiling, happy faces have been a constant feature within their Physical Education lessons during the past year. Being fun, and being enjoyed are essential elements in the lessons if whole-hearted, enthusiastic participation is to be achieved.

Movement Skills Training

1–6 Partners have to agree the same three words which each will use as the basis for an end of year feelings dance. The words express feelings and are to reflect on the three stages of social development of the early stage, middle stage and final stage in their current school year. For example, the words might be 'lonely, shy; more confident, outgoing; and exuberantly happy with companions, or sagging, dejected at the thought of being away from friends for a while'. Expressing the three stage-by-stage feelings through bodily actions is a difficult challenge and each observing partner will need to consider 'Were the actions clear? Were the body shapes full and clear? Was the timing good or was it too rushed, or too long? Was the amount of effort and body tension right?' The teacher's 'Watch your partner's dance after your advice. Then I will ask you to put your hands up if you thought your partner had really improved after your coaching. I might ask you to explain what it

was that was better' focuses pupils attention on the need to reflect on a performance to spread good practice and improve standards.

Feelings Dance

1–5 Percussion-playing partners accompany the three actions, each with a still start and finish position and held shape, with percussionists responsible for the timing of each action. Couples watch couples to guess what the three actions are, after seeing both partners perform. Several successfully expressive couples then demonstrate to share their ideas.

Games

Introduction to Games

The near-total disappearance of out-of-school play – due to hours spent watching television and videos, playing computer games, traffic increase, reported attacks on children and parental concern when children are out of sight – means that regular and vigorous physical lessons where girls and boys move, share, play and learn together are more important than ever if our children are to achieve anything like their potential physical, social, emotional and intellectual development.

Primary school Physical Education lessons are doubly rewarding. First of all, they satisfy the natural biological need for movement in growing, naturally active children, providing pleasure, satisfaction and a healthy outlet for restless, surplus energy. The sense of wellbeing and achievement inspired by enjoyable activity can enhance the quality of school life and childhood. Secondly, the wide range of skills practised and learned will be remembered by the body for a great many years, giving continued pleasure and potentially a lifelong involvement in enjoyable, sociable and healthy physical activities.

The following lesson plans and notes aim to help teachers and schools with a wide variety of material for lesson content, development and progression. The lessons take account of the nature of the weather, with lively running or invasion games throughout the winter, and the less vigorous net/wall and striking/fielding games during warmer months. Each lesson is repeated three or four times to allow plenty of time for the planning, the practising and improving, and the evaluating which are essential elements in good practice in the National Curriculum (NC).

Games equipment

The lesson plans in this book assume that schools have, or are planning to have, the following items of equipment: 30 large balls; 30 hockey sticks; 30 small balls; 6 playground hockey balls; 6 rugby balls; 6 20-cm foam balls; 2 sets netball apparatus; 8 marker cones; playground chalk; 30 short-tennis rackets; 30 outdoor short-tennis balls; 15 playbats; 30 skipping ropes; 6 7-m skipping ropes for group skipping and to make 'nets' when tied between netball posts or chairs; 15 1-m hoops; 6 relay batons; 6 rubber quoits; 6 beanbags; 1 set stoolball apparatus; 1 set Kwik Cricket apparatus.

Games in the playground

All the lessons in this book are planned for the school playground where most primary and middle school games teaching now takes place. Precious time spent travelling to a field; the high cost of coach travel; a wet, muddy surface for much of the year; the need for expensive footwear; and a playing surface on which it is difficult to practise the variety of activities and small-sided games we are required to offer, have all combined to make the school's own playground the setting for the games programme in most schools in preference to a playing field.

Each rectangular third of the netball court is clearly marked with painted lines that should last for several years; these thirds are an ideal size for the three different games which are the climax of each lesson.

Lesson length

The following lessons are broken down into 30- and 45-minute sessions. Where a school allocates the recommended two hours per week for Physical Education, it is usually timetabled as a 1-hour Games lesson, and half-hour lessons for Gymnastic Activities and Dance. If a teacher feels strongly that he or she would like the class to have a movement lesson on as many days of the week as possible, the games hour can become two 30-minute lessons, giving the children an activity lesson on four days per week.

It must be emphasised that the most important part of the lesson is the final group practices and small-sided games which should never be cut short. The teacher needs to count back on his or her watch to check the time at which this main part of the lesson is due to begin, and ensure that it does begin promptly or even early.

The playground 'classroom' and safety

At the very beginning of each year the class must be made aware that the extent of their outdoor 'classroom' or teaching space is the netball court. They must always remain within its outer lines while taking part in the practices that make up the beginning and middle parts of the lesson.

When all members of the class are so contained the teacher can easily see and be seen, be totally in control, and not need to raise and strain his or her voice by shouting to be heard over great distances.

If the school has only one netball court, each of the three games, practices or activities of the final part of the lesson is accommodated in one of the marked thirds of the court. If the school has a second court, a part or the whole of this court can be used to provide more space where it seems sensible, such as in the warming-up activities, the skills practices, and for one of the more lively running games.

A teacher's checklist of safe practices will include:

❍ sensible, safe clothing with no watches, jewellery, rings, long trousers that catch heels, or unbunched hair

❍ good supervision by the teacher whose circulation, mainly on the outside looking in, means that the majority of the class can be seen at all times, with few behind his or her back

❍ good teaching, which aims to develop skilful, well-controlled, safe movement

❍ good behaviour with a tradition of quiet tongues and feet, and instant responses to instructions

❍ an awareness of danger points such as fences, walls, seats, or steps into buildings. These must be avoided by the fast-moving, dodging and chasing children who must remain inside the lines of the netball courts.

Classification of games

In planning an all-year-round Games programme, and to satisfy NC requirements, it is necessary to understand the three groupings into which games can be divided.

Group 1: Invasion or running games

Skills: throwing or striking; catching or collecting; carrying or propelling.
In invasion games such as football, netball, hockey, basketball, rugby and lacrosse, two equal teams compete and the playing area is shared. Players try to advance the ball, eventually to aim to score a goal.

Invasion games, with their possibility of continuous action, are popular and include our best-known and most frequently played winter games. They are exciting and vigorous because of the element of chasing and being chased by opponents who share the same playing area with you.

However, running games are difficult to play well because of the need to outwit close-marking opponents and to co-operate with team-mates in passing and receiving to advance self and ball towards the opponents' goal – a combination of skills calling for a large measure of social and intellectual maturity in addition to physical skill of quite a high level.

Modifications of invasion/running games must be used to keep the number of players per team down to 2 to 5 at the most. A small area needing little territorial advancement of players is essential. The scoring act has to be simple, such as arriving on the goal line with the ball in your possession. A variety of ways to score is recommended to open up the game and prevent the defenders dominating. In touch rugby, for example, the scoring act could include placing the ball down over the opponents' end line as usual, or passing to a team-mate standing on the line, or bouncing the ball in one of two hoops in the corners of the opponents' half.

Group 2: Net/wall games

Skills: striking and aiming as in games such as short-tennis, tennis, volleyball, quoits and badminton.
The 'net' can simply be a painted or chalk line marked on the playground, long skipping ropes tied between netball posts or chairs, or a light net tied between posts or chairs.

Net games are the least complicated of the three types of games and they are the only group where you are not restricted to using a ball. Shuttlecocks, quoits and beanbags as well as balls can be the objects struck, thrown or aimed over the net or line. The court is small with the two teams on separate areas with the minimum of distraction. Teamwork is simple and 'singles' can be played. Little time is wasted and long rallies of continuous play can be engaged in with the ball, quoit, beanbag or shuttlecock being easily reached by the receiver. The target to aim at beyond the net is a generously large one.

Because of their more static, less vigorous nature, net games are more suitable for warmer weather from late spring until autumn.

For most primary schools, the net/wall group of games is limited to net games because they do not have a games wall adjacent to where games are taught. Where there is such a wall, children can play by themselves, or with or against a partner, kicking, heading, throwing, batting or striking with hockey stick, hand or racket.

Group 3: Striking/fielding games

Skills: striking, bowling, throwing, catching, collecting, aiming.
In games such as cricket, rounders and stoolball, the one or two players batting are wholly concerned with striking and they compete against all of the fielding side, who are concerned with bowling, throwing, catching, fielding, aiming and collecting the ball. The striking of the ball is similar to the striking in net games but made more difficult

because the ball usually approaches the batting player more quickly, either through the air directly or after bouncing up from the ground.

Fielders require a wide range of skills to catch or collect all varieties of approaching balls, fast, slow, high, on ground, bouncing unpredictably, coming towards you, or moving at an angle to catcher or fielder. Unfortunately, with young, inexpert children where the batting is poor, weak or erratic, the whole game becomes stagnant, inactive, boring and unphysical with little action to keep the fielding side interested, busy and excited.

Batting games should be played in small groups of 3, 4 or 5 where 'tip-and-run' or 'non-stop cricket' is used to stimulate action among the whole group who continuously change over the roles of bowler, batter, backstop and fielder.Batting games, with their potential for inactivity, particularly among the young and inexperienced, are more suitable for warmer weather during late spring, summer and early autumn.

(15-a-side rounders, often with the teacher bowling, which abounds during the summer term, is the antithesis of all that good Physical Education stands for. It is neither physical nor educational.)

National Curriculum requirements or Games – Key Stage 2: the main features

'The Government believes that two hours of physical activity a week, including the National Curriculum for Physical Education and extra-curricular activities, should be an aspiration for all schools. This applies to all key stages.'

Programme of Study   Pupils should be taught to:

a   play and make up small-sided and modified competitive net, striking/fielding and invasion games
b   use skills and tactics and apply basic principles suitable for attacking and defending
c   work with others to organise and keep the games going.

Attainment Target   Pupils should be able to demonstrate that they can:

a   select and use skills, actions and ideas appropriately, applying them with co-ordination and control
b   when performing, draw on what they know about tactics and strategy
c   compare and comment on skills and ideas used in own work by modifying and refining skills and techniques.

Main NC Headings when considering assessment, progression and expectation

Planning: Performing and participating in a thoughtful, well-organised way is the result of good planning, which takes place before and during performance. Subsequent performances will be influenced by the planning that also takes place after reflecting on the success or otherwise of the activity. Where planning standards are considered to be satisfactory, there is evidence of: (a) thinking ahead; (b) good judgements and decisions; (c) good understanding; (d) originality; (e) consideration for others; (f) positive qualities such as enthusiasm, whole-heartedness and the capacity for working and practising hard to achieve.

Performing and improving performance: We are fortunate in Physical Education because of the visual nature of the activities. It is easy to see, note and remember how pupils perform, demonstrating skill and versatility. Where standards of performing are satisfactory there is evidence of: (a) neatness, accuracy and 'correctness'; (b) skilfulness and versatility; (c) the ability to remember and repeat; (d) safe, successful outcomes; (e) originality of solutions; (f) ability to do more than one thing at a time, linking a series of actions with increasing fluency, accuracy, control and skill; (g) ability to make sudden adjustments as needed; (h) pleasure from participation; (i) a clear understanding of what was required.

Evaluating/reflecting: Evaluation is intended to inform further planning and preparation by helping both performers and spectators with guidance and ideas for altering, adapting, extending and improving performances. Where standards in evaluating are satisfactory, pupils are able to: (a) observe accurately; (b) identify the parts of a performance that they liked; (c) pick out the main features being demonstrated; (d) make comparisons between two performances; (e) reflect on the accuracy of the work; (f) comment on the quality of the movement, using simple terms; (g) suggest ways in which the work might be improved; (h) express pleasure in a performance.

Year 3 Games programme

Pupils should be able to:

Autumn	Spring	Summer
1 Respond quickly to instructions and follow relevant rules.	**1** Continue to develop skill and versatility in sending, receiving and travelling with a ball.	**1** Practise to develop the skills of striking/fielding and net games, individually, in pairs and in small groups or teams.
2 Share space sensibly for own and others' safety.	**2** Practise skills individually, with a partner and in small practices and games.	**2** Perform confidently, with the ability to make quick decisions.
3 Understand dangers of unsuitable clothing, footwear and jewellery.	**3** Show safety awareness in games activities, particularly in sharing limited space in fast-moving games and practices.	**3** Play and create small-sided versions of recognised net and striking/fielding games, sharing decisions on scoring systems, the main rules and how to re-start.
4 Improve skills learned previously, in sending, receiving and travelling with a ball.	**4** Develop neat footwork with quick reactions to avoid others and to evade close-marking opponents.	**4** Discuss good sporting attitudes and recognise the need for rules regarding size of areas and effective boundaries.
5 Improve passing, then running into a space to receive a pass.	**5** Plan, make up and play own games with set limits and agreed rules and scoring systems.	**5** Understand common skills and principles in net and striking/fielding games, e.g. 'good length' ball in tennis or cricket; moving early to be still and ready to catch in cricket or hit in tennis.
6 Practise to improve in a well-planned, thoughtful way.	**6** Learn, habitually, to move to a new space after passing a ball, often 'faking' to pass or run the other way.	
7 Understand the use of side-steps, direction and speed changes to evade a close-marking opponent.	**7** Understand and improve '1-on-1' marking to keep 'in line' between an opponent and his/her target line.	**6** Understand differing roles and duties as members of teams and groups in net and striking/fielding games, e.g. bat, bowl, field, keep wickets.
8 Apply skills in simple games.	**8** Respond safely, alone and with others, to challenging tasks, often to 'keep going, non-stop, to improve and keep warm'.	**7** Enjoy playing co-operatively to develop skill, and playing competitively to test skill.
9 Co-operate with a partner to develop skills in co-operative and competitive situations.	**9** Experience small-sided (1 v 1 up to 4 v 4) games, often of the half-court, '3 lives' variety.	**8** Observe demonstrations with interest and suggest ways to improve performance.
10 Move vigorously to maintain warmth in colder weather.	**10** Make simple judgements on own and others' performance.	
11 Improve dodging and marking skills in games situations.		
12 Show adaptability by quick responses to the unexpected.		
13 Observe others working and answer questions on work seen.		
14 Reflect with a partner on how to improve own created games.		
15 Suggest improvements to games – extra ways to score; how to re-start; and one main rule.		

Lesson Plan 1 • 30-45 minutes
September

Warm-up and Footwork Practices
4—6 minutes

1 Show me your best and quietest running, with bent arms going straight forwards and back, and knees lifting and pushing well forwards.

2 Keep running. When I call a number, make a circle, hands joined with that number of people, as quickly as you can. Let's see who is not in a circle or last to join one. (3! 2! 4!; intersperse numbers with good running.)

Skills Practices: with playbats or rackets and small balls
8—12 minutes

Individual practices

1 Walking with ball balanced on bat or racket.

2 Walking, striking gently and catching ball on bat or racket. Can you do this gently and rotate wrist each time to produce a forehand and a backhand position?

3 Strike up, let bounce; strike up higher, let bounce; strike up even higher, let bounce.

Partner practices

1 Walk beside your partner, one of you with ball balanced on bat or racket. Can you transfer ball to other bat or racket?

2 Four metres apart, bowl slowly underarm to bounce for partner to hit back for an easy catch by bowler.

Group practices and Small-sided Games
18—27 minutes

Bat, racket or hand tennis over rope 'net'

Co-operate with partner in striking ball gently just short of partner for easy return. Keep your best score. If this is too difficult, one can throw gently for other to strike.

One hoop each

Place hoop on ground. Show me how you can use it for balancing activities. Pick up hoop and show me how you can use it on the move. Bowling? Throwing and catching? Skipping?

One beanbag among 3

2 v 1, where the 2, about 3 metres apart, interpass to outwit the 1. Emphasise 'Pass and move sideways'; 'Fake to pass; hold; then pass'; 'Hands forwards in ready position to receive beanbag.'

Games

Teaching notes and NC guidance
Development over 4–5 lessons

Lesson's main emphases:

a The NC general requirement that pupils should be taught to be physically active and respond readily to instructions.

b Safe practice in dress; immediate responses; sharing space co-operatively; and remembering that games are meant to be good fun, to teach us worthwhile skills and help us physically, not cause us hurt or accident.

Equipment: 30 small bat shapes or rackets, and 30 small balls; 10 hoops; 3 beanbags; 1 long rope as a 'net'.

Warm-up and Footwork Practices

Emphasise that in good running you do not follow anyone, and you do not continually run anti-clockwise where everyone follows everyone. (Very common in primary schools.) Stop class occasionally anyway to practise responding immediately to a command. Ask them to move 1 or 2 steps away from anyone near them, to be seen standing in their own space. In good, quiet running, we lift our heels and knees, and we run on straight lines, not curving around, following others.

Skills Practices: with playbats or rackets and small balls

Individual practices

1 Racket is held quite high at about mid-chest height so that you can have a good look at the ball while balancing it.

2 Use the wrist to move the bat or racket to propel the ball, not the elbow or the shoulder, which would give too strong a strike. 'Forehand' means palm up; 'backhand' means knuckles up.

3 Practise the striking up to bounce on the spot, then on the move when ready. Once again, use wrist action and 'feel' how much is needed for the different heights.

Partner practices

1 Demonstrate with good couples who transfer ball from bat to bat slowly, near eye level, on the move, with wrists doing the work.

2 'Bowl low and slow' for easy returns and catches. Six bowls per partner, then change duties. Bowl to partner's forehand side for easier return.

Group Practices and Small-sided Games

Bat, racket or hand tennis over rope 'net'.

Make low 'net' by tying long skipping ropes between netball posts or chairs. Use hand, bat or racket as necessary to ensure success and allow reasonable rallies to be achieved.

One hoop each

Hoop balance: walk forwards, back, sideways or on hands and feet. Try skipping with hoop swinging side to side by 1-hand action.

One beanbag between three

'1' can be passive, not trying to intercept, if class is inexperienced in 'outwitting' an enthusiastic, chasing defender. Change the '1' over often.

Lesson Plan 2 • 30-45 minutes
October

Warm-up and Footwork Practices
4—6 minutes

1 Run freely and quietly, visiting all parts of our playground classroom. Use side-steps or direction changes to avoid others coming towards you.

2 All-against-all tag. Count how many others you touch and count how often you are touched. Be gentle with your touching. No hard, dangerous pushing.

Skills Practices: with large balls
8—12 minutes

Individual practices

1 Walk, throwing and catching the ball above head height with both hands.

2 Walk, bouncing ball with fingertips, with left and right hands, and with changes of direction and speed.

Partner practices

Throw ball to one side of partner who is moving into space to receive it. Pass; then move into a space to receive when partner is ready to pass.

Invent a Skills Practice in 2s
3—5 minutes

Can you and your partner invent a practice to develop the habit of running into a space, ready to receive a pass, and the habit of always looking for someone moving before making your pass? (For example, catcher develops a signal to use before running into a space. Point with 1 hand, then go in that direction, or run with 1 hand up-stretched as target for passer to aim at.)

Group Practices and Small-sided Games
15—22 minutes

Large ball among 4

2 v 2 in half area, with attackers having 3 'lives' to score on opponents' line. Decide the scoring system, how to advance the ball, and the main rule. Change over after 3 attacks or 'lives'.

1 bat, 1 ball among 4

Non-stop cricket in half of area.

Skipping rope each

Practise, revise, show me how well you can skip. Quiet, slow, with little hand action. Keep going, as a group, for 1 minute, showing good variety, e.g. on the spot and moving; feet together or one after the other; in different directions.

Games

Teaching notes and NC guidance
Development over 4–5 lessons

Lesson's main emphases:

a The NC requirement to improve the skills of sending and receiving a ball, and to make up and play their own practices.

b Appreciating how much we need and depend on a partner or a small group to provide the unexpected and the unpredicted, which are elements that give games their attraction and their potential for excitement.

Equipment: 30 large balls; 2 bats, small balls, cones or wickets; 10 skipping ropes.

Warm-up and Footwork Practices

1 Visit all parts of our playground classroom – the ends, sides, corners and the middle. Look out for and avoid other runners.

2 In all-against-all tag, or 'it', stop the game every 12 seconds or so to calm them down, re-assert control, and to check on 'Which good chasers caught 5 or more? Which good dodgers were not touched at all?' Demonstrate with a good dodger being pursued.

Skills Practices: with large balls

Individual practices

1 Practise on the move to keep class warm and to give games-like conditions as we continually work among and keep aware of other movers. Catch with both hands and grab ball in to yourself, securely, carefully watching ball the whole time.

2 Fingertip dribbling, as in basketball, is a good way of 'travelling with a ball'. Emphasise 'use your wrists strongly, not your elbows or your shoulders, as you dribble the ball, and practise changing hands, height and speeds, for variety.'

Partner practices

'Pass, then move! Give, then go!' will be said continually so that the passer comes to expect the previous thrower to be moving into a space to be available for the next pass.

Invent a Skills Practice

Planning, performing and reflecting on the practice you and your partner have worked together to create, helps to make you more thoughtful participants and better observers generally.

Group Practices and Small-sided Games

Large ball among 4

In 2-versus-2, you can score by touching ball on line, by passing to a partner on the line, by making 3 good passes, etc. A 'life' is lost when the opponents steal the ball from the attackers.

1 bat, 1 ball among 4

In non-stop cricket, the batter must run around cone and back every time a hit is made. All change duties often for variety. Rules to get batter 'out' in various ways should develop by mutual agreement.

Skipping rope each

Encourage 'can your whole group plan and demonstrate a good variety within your non-stop skipping? Use eyes as well as legs.'

Lesson Plan 3 • 30-45 minutes
November

Warm-up and Footwork Practices
4—6 minutes

1   Run quietly and well without following anyone. Show me slow running when near others or in a corner, and sprint running when there is plenty of space.

2   Tag, with 6 chasers wearing bands, who can catch you if you are within the lines. You can 'hide' on any line. When caught, put on a band and become a chaser.

Skills Practices: with large balls
8—12 minutes

Individual practices

1   All dribble, slowly, football fashion. Listen for my 'Stop!' when you will bring your ball under control as quickly as possible, with foot on top of ball. 'Stop!'

2   Do the same again, feeling which part or parts of your feet can dribble the ball with most control. Stop!

3   Push the ball gently a couple of metres ahead of you, then run to control it, and repeat. Use dribbling taps to take you into a space.

Partner practices

1   Shadow dribbling, with the leader dribbling to a certain pattern for the following partner to copy. Leader changes over after about 3 repetitions of the pattern.

2   Four metres apart, pass to your partner who has moved to a space in which to receive your pass. Receive on count 1; move ball forwards ready for pass on count 2 (watching for partner's move); pass on count 3; then move to a space to receive on count 4.

Invent a Skills Practice in 2s
3—5 minutes

Can you and your partner invent a practice or game to develop the skills of dribbling, passing or receiving that we have been doing? (For example, 8 metres apart with a line in between, one dribbles 4 metres to line, passes to stationary partner, then returns to own starting line as partner repeats the activity.)

Group Practices and Small-sided Games
15—22 minutes

Dribbling-tag, large ball each
All try to score points by touching other football dribblers. Control ball while tagging.

Large ball among 4, 2 v 2
Attackers score by bouncing ball in 1 of 2 hoops in the corners. Half pitch area. After 3 attacks, change duties. Decide on main rule.

Large ball between 2
Including chest and bounce passing, show me ways to send ball accurately to your partner (e.g. kick, head, throw, volley).

Games

Teaching notes and NC guidance
Development over 4–5 lessons

Lesson's main emphases:

a The NC requirement to improve the skills of sending, receiving and travelling with a ball, and making up and playing their own games or practices.

b An awareness of the need for all to work hard to make our lessons into 'scenes of busy activity' as we move into winter and colder weather. We want maximum, vigorous physical participation and a minimum of 'dead spots' when no-one is working.

Equipment: 30 large balls; coloured bands; 4 hoops.

Warm-up and Footwork Practices

1 Changing running speed is also an excellent dodge in Games to evade a close marking opponent.

2 In tag, where you cannot be caught on a line, the class will probably agree a reasonable time limit (about 5 seconds) for those 'refugees' who linger on their lines unsportingly.

Skills Practices: with large balls

Individual practices

1 Ask class to look at a good group and tell you which part or parts of the feet being used seem to work most successfully, both for 'travelling with the ball' and for quick control.

2 Encourage them to practise with left and right feet.

3 Push it into a space where you won't impede others or be impeded in your follow-up run to regain control.

Partner practices

1 In shadow dribbling, the performer has to remember the sequence to repeat it. The follower has to recognise the 2 or 3 parts concerned to be able to repeat them in the right order.

2 'Pass and move. Give and go. Pass and move into a space' will be heard over and over again in Games lessons and teaching. It is hoped that the 'give and go' pattern becomes an ingrained habit. A passer is expected to move into a new space to be ready for a return throw.

Group Practices and Small-sided Games

Dribbling-tag, large ball each

In dribbling-tag, do not allow chasers to leave their ball and tag someone. Gentle tags. No rough pushing.

Large ball among 4, 2 v 2

In 2-versus-2, the game is one way only, half pitch, with same team having 3 'lives' or attacks, then becoming the defenders. Send the ball to your partner in a variety of ways – straight chest to chest, bounce, after a fake – then move to a new space to help. In deciding their main rule, emphasise that the rule aims to keep the game fair for both teams, and to keep the game flowing. In cold weather, running side by side, passing rugby style, is good for keeping you warm.

Lesson Plan 4 • 30-45 minutes
December

Warm-up and Footwork Practices
4—6 minutes

1 Follow-the-leader, walking, running and jumping over lines. When you think you can repeat your partner's sequence, ask to become the new leader.

2 In pairs, marker shadows dodger. On 'Stop!' both freeze to see who is the winner; the dodger clear, or marker still within touching distance. Change over.

Skills Practices: with large balls
8—12 minutes

Indvidual practices

1 Run, ball held low, like a rugby player. Run with arms swinging naturally from side to side, making fake passes to each side.

2 When I call 'Change!' put your ball down on the ground with a rugby-try scoring action, and run and pick up another ball. Use two hands for both actions. (Teacher can add to the fun of this practice by removing some of the balls so that not all succeed in finding one to pick up.)

Partner practices

1 Run side by side, passing rugby style, sideways to your partner. Pass across the leg nearer to your partner and just ahead of him, so that he runs on to the ball.

2 One of you stands still while the other runs around in a circle about 3 metres away. The still partner throws in front of the running partner, who carries the ball a few strides before passing the ball back. Change duties often.

Invent a Skills Practice in 2s
3—5 minutes

Half of class still have a ball. Can anyone invent a game that uses carrying the ball and dodging to avoid being touched? (For example, those without try to touch a ball being carried to gain one – having a ball is good. Or those with ball could touch someone without who then must take it – not having a ball is good.)

Group Practices and Small-sided Games
15—22 minutes

Rugby-touch, 4 v 4, large ball among 8

Score by passing to team-mate catcher near opponents' line or by touching down on end line.

Invent a game, 1 v 1, large ball between 2

Using part of line and 1 ball, invent a football dribbling game. Decide main rule.

10 hockey sticks, 7 balls

Three pupils, with stick but no ball, try to take one from the dribbling 7.

Games

Teaching notes and NC guidance
Development over 4–5 lessons

Lesson's main emphases:

a The NC general requirement to make appropriate decisions quickly and plan their responses.

b Using the leg muscles vigorously in invasion or running games and practices, which are appropriate in winter to warm us and keep us warm. In addition, good responses and excellent behaviour become even more important to ensure that the lesson is seldom stopped.

Equipment: 30 large balls, including as many rugby balls as possible; 10 hockey sticks and 7 small balls (playground hockey type if available).

Warm-up and Footwork Practices

1 In follow-the-leader, aim to be so good that you and your partner can perform almost in unison, stepping together.

2 In dodge-and-mark, encourage, coach and demonstrate good dodges, fakes of head or shoulders, and direction changes. Discourage high-speed, dangerous sprints by dodgers. Be very firm against the cheating, commonplace in this game, by those who do not stop immediately you shout 'Stop!'

Skills Practices: with large balls

Individual practices

1 A fake pass is one that looks as if it is going to happen but doesn't.

2 The 'Change!' balls practice is good fun, calls for a quick response, and is an excellent rugby practice.

Partner practices

Aim to give your partner an easy two-handed catch to run on to by aiming just in front of his chest. Turn your upper body right around to face the target, letting both arms follow through towards the target as you pass the ball.

Invent a Skills Practice in 2s

One of the class, particularly if he has invented the game suggested, can shout 'Change!' to change the aim of the game from having to not having a ball in your possession.

Group Practices and Small-sided Games

Rugby-touch, 4 v 4, large ball among 8

In rugby-touch, the choice of scoring ideas produces more goals. The teams can be challenged to add to these. Teams must agree how to re-start after a score, and one main rule to keep the game fair to both teams.

Invent a game, 1 v 1, large ball between 2

In 1 v 1 dribbling to score at a line, decide how to score, how to restrict the defender, how to restart, and the one main rule. The defender might be required to stay within a metre of the line.

10 hockey sticks, 7 balls

Teacher will spend much time with the hockey group, teaching the correct, safe way to hold stick low and in front at all times.

Lesson Plan 5 ● 30-45 minutes
January

Warm-up and Footwork Practices
4–6 minutes

1 Jogging is an easy, quiet form of running, with arms hanging low and heels not as high as in normal running. Practise easy jogging at a speed you think you can easily keep going for 2 minutes.

2 10-points tag, all against all. All have 10 points to start with. Each time someone touches you, you lose a point. (N.B. Gentle touching. No pushing. Check who has the most points left and who caught the most, after 12–15 second game.)

Skills Practices: with hockey sticks and small balls
8–12 minutes

Individual practices

1 Run, with stick in right hand by side like a suitcase. Hold stick in the middle, flat side to left and head pointing forwards.

2 When I call 'Change!' place left hand on top of stick, leaving right hand where it is. Carry in front, head of stick near ground as if about to receive a ball. Keep running. (Change between '1' and '2' several times.)

3 With your ball now, keep the flat side of the stick forwards and slightly to the right. Push the ball gently in front of you, along a straight line.

Partner practices

1 Your partner is 3 metres away. Dribble around your partner and back to your starting place. Push ball to partner who repeats the practice.

2 Walk side by side, gently sending ball in front of each other.

Group Practices and Small-sided Games
18–27 minutes

Hockey stick and ball each

Walk with ball 'glued' to stick. When you see a space about 2–3 metres ahead, push-pass ball into the space. Run after ball and repeat. Emphasise low stick in front of you at all times. No high follow-through.

Large ball among 4, 2 v 2, half pitch

Attackers try to score, rugby style, by usual touch down over opponents' line, by a pass to partner on line, or into one or more hoops which can be additional scoring systems. When touched by defender, you must pass the ball.

Large ball between 2

Allowing one bounce on the ground in between hits, keep your best score in juggling the ball to keep it up and bouncing, using foot, thigh or head. A sort of football-tennis on the spot.

Games

Teaching notes and NC guidance
Development over 4–5 lessons

Lesson's main emphases:

a The NC requirement to play fairly, compete honestly and demonstrate good sporting behaviour.

b 'Keeping going', as in our jogging start, and in our near non-stop lesson. This is something children do not experience sufficiently often, according to a survey by Exeter University. Heart health is always an aim of a good, vigorous Physical Education lesson, particularly now, when children's sedentary lifestyles are so lacking in vigorous play and exercise.

Equipment: 30 hockey sticks and small balls; 7 large balls.

Warm-up and Footwork Practices

1 Find, feel, and almost hear your own rhythm in your jogging. 'Jog, jog, jog, jog; 1, 2, 3, 4.' There is little forward body lean. Hands and heels are low and 'easy'.

2 In 10-points tag, encourage good dodges with head and shoulder fakes, quick changes of direction and changes of speed.

Skills Practices: with hockey sticks and small bats

Individual practices

1 This carry of the stick by your side is safe, unlike running and waving stick about, and means the stick easily comes to hand to play the ball.

2 Stick is carried low and in front when ball is being played or has been played. Side carry alternates safely with forwards carry.

3 Straight line push forwards is done by placing the stick behind the ball then giving it a push. There is no long, dangerous, out of sight backswing.

Partner practices

1 Walk and dribble to start with, passing partner with your left shoulder. Send ball to partner by placing stick behind ball, then pushing, not hitting or slapping it.

2 Side by side, dribble for 3 or 4 touches, then place stick down at back of ball and push it just ahead of partner who keeps moving forwards to receive it easily. Turn and pass to other side.

Group Practices and Small-sided Games

Hockey stick and ball each

More time for individual hockey dribble and push ahead practice to reinforce, adapt and improve the earlier attempts.

Large ball among 4, 2 v 2 half pitch

Half pitch, 2 v 2, rugby-touch games require good co-operation between the attackers and skilful, accurate passing. The touch by the defender must be gentle with no dangerous pushing. To keep the game interesting with lots of scoring opportunities, other ideas for scoring are always being looked for.

Large ball between 2

Both players must keep 'on their toes' to be able to move quickly to where the next bounce is going to happen. Players can agree to alternate hits or to a little, individual rally, then 'Over to you, partner.'

Lesson Plan 6 • 30-45 minutes
February

Warm-up and Footwork Practices
4—6 minutes

1 All in half of third of netball court. Using changes of speed and direction, and running on the spot, try to share this small area without bumping. Go slowly when crowded, faster when room.

2 Dodge and mark to one end of area so defenders stay 'in line' between partner and target line to impede progress. Change duties often. Defenders keep feet apart, hips low for 'boxer's shuffle' sideways and backwards.

Skills Practices: with large balls
8—12 minutes

Partner practices

1 3 metres apart, chest pass to partner with both hands and then move sideways into a space to receive the return pass.

2 Bounce pass to partner, moving to new space for return pass. Aim to bounce ball about 1 metre in front of partner.

3 Fake a pass one way, then chest or bounce pass to partner the other way.

Small group practices in 3s

1 2-versus-1 passing where the '1' is passive, keeping between the '2', but not trying to intercept. Change over '1' often.

2 3s, team passing where the person with the ball passes to a team-mate who has just moved, or better, signalled and moved into a space about 3 metres from ball-handler.

Invent a Skills Practice or Simple Game in 3s
3—5 minutes

Can you invent a game with 1 ball to improve and develop the skill of passing and moving? (For example, each has a number 1, 2, or 3. Ball passed 1 to 2 to 3 to 1 to 2 to 3. Next receiver has to call his number, signal low before running to a space if bounce pass wanted or with high arm for a chest pass. Fakes can be added before run to a space.)

Group Practices and Small-sided Games
15—22 minutes

Hoop-ball, 2 v 1, half pitch

Attackers score by bouncing ball in one of defenders' hoops. 3 'lives' or attacks each, then change duties.

2 v 1, hockey stick, 1 ball

'2s' try to pass to each other. '1' is passive, simply trying to keep between the other 2.

Invent a game, large ball, 1 v 1 at a line

Attacker tries to cross line, dribbling by hand or foot. What is main rule? How is goalkeeper restricted? How many attacks each?

Games

Teaching notes and NC guidance
Development over 4–5 lessons

Lesson's main emphases:

a The NC requirements to explore and understand principles of defence in invasion games and sustain energetic activity.

b Working hard as a team defence with good body positioning and footwork to frustrate the attacking team. The opponents will find it hard to score if you keep 'in line' at all times.

Equipment: 15 large balls; 10 hockey sticks; 3 playground-hockey balls; 4 hoops.

Warm-up and Footwork Practices

1 Neat footwork and quick reactions are needed to prevent bumps.

2 Pairs can play across thirds, line to line, with attacker trying to pass defender to arrive on target line. In the low, defensive 'shuffle', feet never cross or come together.

Skills Practices: with large balls

Partner practices

1 We 'pass and move into a space' because that is the way to advance yourself and the ball in invasion/running games, and to keep warm in winter, with constant movement.

2 The bounce pass is used to push ball under the arms of a close marking defender, particularly one who is taller than you.

3 A fake, dummy or decoy pass can be made by moving head, foot or shoulders and ball in one direction, stopping suddenly without throwing, then passing the other way as an unexpected move.

Small group practices in 3s

1 In 2-versus-1, the passive '1' is still very lively, moving fast to keep between the passers, forcing them to move sideways and forwards to be open to receive a pass.

2 In team passing in 3s, you will not receive a pass if you have not just moved to a new space to encourage such movement.

Invent a Skills Practice or Simple Game in 3s

In a small rectangle with an end line, the 2 with the ball could have 3 'lives' or attacks against '1', who has to defend hard because outnumbered, guarding the goal line.

Group Practices and Small-sided Games

Hoop-ball, 2 v 1, half pitch

'3 lives', half pitch hoop-ball produces lots of goals because of the 2 separate target hoops. Defenders cannot crowd around as when there is only one goal target. Ask children to decide on how to re-start after a goal, the one main rule, and any ways to limit either attack or defence for fairness and to keep game moving.

2 v 1, hockey stick, 1 ball

The passive '1' works hard to keep in front of the player with the ball, forcing the receiver to move to one side for the pass.

Invent a game, large ball, 1 v 1 at a line

In 1-versus-1, at a line, invent a game, limiting length of line to about 3 metres, and agree some form of limit on each player.

Lesson Plan 7 • 30-45 minutes
March

Warm-up and Footwork Practices
4—6 minutes

1   Run and jump over lines and carry on running. In a long jump, reach well forwards with front leg. In a high jump, which is slower, reach up with the leading knee.

2   Free-and-caught. 6 chasers wearing bands try to catch others who then stand still, hands on head, until freed by a touch on the elbow from an uncaught player.

Skills Practices: with skipping ropes
8—12 minutes

Individual practices

1   Practise slow, 'double-beat' skipping on the spot. Jump twice for every turn of the rope. Hands turn very slowly and easily.

2   Practise quicker, '1-beat' skipping where rope turns with every jump on the spot.

3   Now practise a favourite way of skipping and travelling.

Partner practices

1   Follow your leader, who will show you a sequence that includes something on the spot and something on the move.

2   Can you copy and move in unison, trying to mirror each other?

Invent a Skills Practice for 2 Skippers
3—5 minutes

Can you and your partner, both skipping to keep active and warm, invent a skipping practice which has very obvious variety? (For example, one skips on the spot, turning anti-clockwise, while the other skips in a clockwise circle around him.)

Group Practices and Small-sided Games
15—22 minutes

Skipping rope between 2 partners

Can you and your partner invent ways to skip together using 1 rope only? One can hold rope for both. Each can hold an end of the rope.

Large ball, hoops and skittles, 4 v 4

Skittle-ball with skittles in 4 corner hoops, giving attackers a choice of goals to aim at. Space out in attack. Keep them guessing with fake passes.

Foam ball among 4, 2 v 2 heading ball across half area

Score by heading ball passed by partner over opponents' goal line. Defenders keep 'in line' to impede attackers. Use bounce passes under arms of defender.

Games

Teaching notes and NC guidance
Development over 4–5 lessons

Lesson's main emphases:

a The NC requirement to work safely with others, particularly as they plan, organise, refine and play their own games.

b Enjoying an interesting, almost non-stop lesson with its varied apparatus and activities, making us feel alive ('Life effervescing within me') and refreshed for our return to the classroom. Nothing else we do in a school day brings us closer together with others than the partner and group activities and games that we do in these lessons.

Equipment: 30 skipping ropes; 1 large ball; 4 hoops and skittles; 2 foam balls.

Warm-up and Footwork Practices

1 In the long jump you can see your front foot reaching out in front of you. In the high jump you can only see your leading knee reaching up in front of you.

2 Keep changing the 6 chasers and encourage the chasers to space themselves out, 2 to each third of the netball court.

Skills Practices: with skipping ropes

Individual practices

1 'Double-beat', slow-motion skipping is a jump as you clear the rope, and a little bounce of feet as rope passes slowly overhead. '1 and; 2 and; 3 and;' where '1' is the jump and the 'and' is the little bounce.

2 In '1-beat' skipping you jump on every count. '1; 2; 3' with a much quicker action of wrists and hands needed.

3 A favourite way of skipping should be one you can continue.

Partner practices

1 In follow-the-leader, keep about 3 metres behind leader to avoid swinging rope over partner's head! Staying back also helps the observer to have a better look at the leader's leg actions.

2 'Moving in unison' can be on the spot or on the move.

Invent a Skills Practice for 2 Skippers

The variety requested can be produced by using different actions, going in different directions, varying speeds, on the spot and moving.

Group Practices and Small-sided Games

Skipping rope between 2 partners

Remember to demonstrate the varied ideas for partner skipping with 1 rope. This will extend and develop the class repertoire (and the teacher's repertoire) in this lively activity.

Large ball, hoops and skittles, 4 v 4

In skittle-ball, encourage 2 of the team to play forwards as target players for the rear court bringers of the ball to pass to. Good 'in line', vigorous, chasing defending should be praised, and an excellent team can be used for a demonstration.

Foam ball among 4, 2 v 2 heading ball across half area

In heading-ball in half area, emphasise that a player on opponents' line can pass back to running partner for good header or head large foam ball passed forwards to him for shot at goal.

Lesson Plan 8 • 30-45 minutes
April

Warm-up and Footwork Practices
4—6 minutes

1 Follow your leader, who includes some hurdling actions over a line and some scissors jumping, swinging leg up and over a line.

2 Stand beside a partner, spaced well away from all other couples. On my signal, one races to touch all 4 outside lines and back to touch partner who does the same thing. Go!

Skills Practices: with small balls
8—12 minutes

Individual practices

1 While walking, throw, clap hands, catch in both hands at eye level.

2 Throw low, throw medium, throw quite high and catch with both hands.

3 Roll ball away from you, run after it, drop down to field with fielding hand and opposite foot forwards, ball at good hand side.

Partner practices

1 Stand facing each other about 3 metres apart, hands forwards ready and feet apart. Throw low (knee), throw medium (waist), and throw high (shoulders).

2 10 metres apart. A rolls ball towards B who runs forwards, then crouches to pick ball up and throw back to A. Change places after 4–6 practices.

Invent a Skills Practice or Simple Game
3—5 minutes

Can you and your partner, with 1 ball, invent a practice or little game to improve and develop your throwing and catching in a very small area? (For example, see how many sets of low, medium and high catches you can make while your partner runs to touch the 4 sides of your third of the netball court.)

Group Practices and Small-sided Games
15—22 minutes

3s, 1 ball and 1 cone

A bowls to B, who bats ball a short distance forwards. A fields ball and throws to stumper C. C then rolls ball back to A. Rotate often.

Long skipping ropes

Teams of 5, skipping practices. Plan the best time to come into and leave the swinging long rope. Aim to have all 3 in skipping.

Quoits, 1 v 1

Rope 'net' at head height, tied between netball posts. If quoit lands on partner's side a point is scored. What is your main rule?

Games

Teaching notes and NC guidance
Development over 4–5 lessons

Lesson's main emphases:

a The NC requirement to make judgements of performance and suggest ways of improving.

b Concentrating on the less physical, less active net and striking/fielding games, which are appropriate in warmer weather.

Equipment: 30 small balls; 2 long skipping ropes; 5 quoits and high rope 'net'.

Warm-up and Footwork Practices

1 In follow-the-leader, emphasise 'Lead your partner into good spaces for your lively jumping.' In hurdling, run straight at the line. In scissors jumping, approach at an angle to the line, which nearer leg swings over.

2 In sprinting to touch all 4 side lines, the quick thinkers will run to 2 diagonally opposite corners, touching the 2 lines that meet in those corners!

Skills Practices: with small balls

Individual practices

1 Clapping puts the hands in a good catching position, cupped near eye level in front of you, where you can see the ball well.

2 The low, medium and high throws for catching practice are all quite low to stop silly high throws that are never caught. 'Low' is waist high; 'medium' is chest high; 'high' is head high only.

3 To field a ball correctly, run and crouch while running beside it, facing the way the ball is rolling. The other ways of running sideways or trying to get past and ahead of it are too slow and awkward.

Partner practices

1 In this stationary throwing and catching practice at different heights, the main points are 'Hands both forwards ready. One foot in front of the other for balance. Close your cupped hands around the ball to stop it bouncing out again.'

2 In running in to field a rolling ball to throw back, crouch with a turn, feet wide with throwing arm side back. Pick up, swing arm back and throw.

Invent a Skills Practice or Simple Game

In addition to the example game, an aiming practice, throwing at a line between you to count direct hits, develops throwing and catching competitively.

Group Practices and Small-sided Games

3s, 1 ball and 1 cone

3s, bowling; batting with hand for greater control; fielding; stumping – restrict these to a very small space, at most half of the group's third of the netball court.

Long skipping rope

You come into the long rope as it hits the ground, swinging away from you. You come out of the rope left as it starts to swing right. With beginners, a low swing to waist height is used.

Quoits, 1 v 1

Throw quoit with 1 hand, catch with 1 or 2. The serve should be made at least 3 metres from the 'net'.

Lesson Plan 9 • 30-45 minutes
May

Warm-up and Footwork Practices
4—6 minutes

1. Run to all parts of the playground, emphasising good lift of leading knee to lengthen your strides.

2. Now emphasise strong, powerful straightening behind you of the driving leg.

3. With a partner, count how many 2-footed long jumps from a standing start your pair needs to cross from side line to opposite side line. Each one jumps from partner's landing spot.

Skills Practices: with short-tennis rackets and balls
8—12 minutes

Individual practices

1. Walk, gently hitting ball up a very short distance.

2. Continue, and can you change the hand position each time, from forehand to backhand to forehand to backhand?

3. Walk, gently hitting ball up and forwards to bounce in front. Run to recover. Repeat.

Partner practices

1. Throw to bounce up for easy forehand return for partner to catch. Striker tries to hit ball from side-on position. Change over every 6 practices. What is your best score out of 6?

2. Using hands, rackets or a mixture of the 2, stand side on to your partner and see how long a rally you can make together.

Invent a Skills Practice or Simple Game
3—5 minutes

With 1 or 2 rackets and balls, can you and your partner invent a game or practice to improve and develop your sending and receiving of the ball? (For example, one stands still, hitting ball up, letting it bounce, hitting it up, while the partner hits it up only and changes from forehand to backhand each time, slowly walking in a circle around the stationary partner. Keep going until one partner's rally breaks down.)

Group Practices and Small-sided Games
15—22 minutes

Short tennis with a partner

Play over low rope 'net' tied to chairs or netball posts. Co-operate to learn and improve forehand stroke.

Non-stop cricket in 4s

Bowler, batter, fielder, wicketkeeper decide on how 'out' and how to score. Play in small area. (N.B. Hit out of small area is 'out').

Athletic activities

Measured, standing long jump. Hurdling practice over canes on low cones. Throw small ball to partner, hitting target line.

Games

Teaching notes and NC guidance
Development over 4–5 lessons

Lesson's main emphases:

a The NC requirements to improve the skills of sending and receiving a ball in net, striking/fielding games, and playing simplified versions of recognised games.

b Athletic activities to practise and develop basic actions in running, throwing and jumping.

c Appreciating that our good habits of practising quietly and thoughtfully, plus being asked often to look at demonstrations and suggest ways of improving, have helped to make us become better, more confident and more versatile performers.

Equipment: 30 short-tennis rackets and small balls; long rope as 'net'; 2 bats, small balls and 2 sets of wickets or 2 cones; 3 canes, 6 low cones.

Warm-up and Footwork Practices

1 Stride length is increased by a higher lift of knee and thigh.

2 Increased power comes from a stronger push by the driving foot.

3 In the partner standing long jumps across the court, the jumper swings arms high above head, swings arms behind back and bends knees ready, then drives forwards with legs and swings arms forwards to help. Partner stands with toes in line with jumping partner's toes, ready to do the next jump.

Skills Practices: with short-tennis rackets and balls

Individual practices

1 In hitting ball up, hold racket at upper chest height, and hit ball up to about head height only.

2 Explain 'forehand and backhand' by showing palm and knuckles side of hand alternately uppermost. Wrist twists quickly to make the changes.

3 In the walking and hitting up practice, 'gently' means using the wrist, not the elbow or shoulder, to move the racket.

Partner practices

1 In partner bowling and batting, tell bowler to throw 'low and slow' to partner's forehand side, to bounce to mid-chest level.

2 'Side on to partner' at moment of strike means that racket is at right angles to partner for a straight hit back.

Invent a Skills Practice or Simple Game

One partner, watched by other, could try tiny forehand and backhand strokes over a line on the playground, shuttling feet from side to side. When rally breaks down, other partner can start. Whose is the best rally?

Group Practices and Small-sided Games

Short Tennis with a partner

The short tennis with a partner can be played with hand, racket or combination, if play with the racket is too difficult for both.

Non-stop cricket in 4s

In non-stop cricket, insist 'ball must stay in your small area.'

Athletic activities

Place a metre stick parallel with the jump in the standing long jump, and draw the take-off line with chalk. Place low cone hurdles far enough apart to allow 3 steps in between. 'Over, 1, 2, 3, over.'

Lesson Plan 10 • 30-45 minutes
June

Warm-up and Footwork Practices
4–6 minutes

Jog around the outside of the marked area (netball court or courts) which we will call the 'track' of about 90 metres. Keep a steady pace for 1 minute, and count your laps and part laps completed. Back in class we can work out how far you jogged, easily, in a minute. Next lesson, you might travel a bit further. Off you go!

Skills Practices: with bat shapes and small balls
8–12 minutes

Individual practices

1   Walk about with your ball balanced on the bat as in an egg and spoon race.

2   Change to gentle batting upwards using your wrist only. No big elbow or shoulder movements. What is your best score?

3   Throw ball up with hand, let it bounce on the ground, bat it up with bat and catch it with 1 hand. Repeat.

Partner practices

Partner A strikes ball from hand to partner B who catches it at various heights and speeds. Have 6 goes each, then change. What is your team's best score out of 12 attempts?

Group Practices and Small-sided Games
18–27 minutes

Tip-and-run cricket in groups of 5

In small area. 1 bowler, 2 batters, 1 wicketkeeper, 1 fielder. The group decide how 'out', how to score, how and when to rotate positions. Bowler tries to make the batter play as he then has to run, giving the chance to catch or run out.

Hand-tennis, 1 v 1, over low rope 'net'

Children decide how to start games, how to score, when ball is out of play, and when to change ends, if at all.

Athletic activities

a   Shuttle relays, 2 teams of 4 or 5

b   Beanbag putting from a line

c   Standing high jump over low cane held by partner.

Teaching notes and NC guidance
Development over 4–5 lessons

Lesson's main emphases:

a The NC requirements to improve the skills of sending, striking and receiving a ball in net and striking/fielding games.

b Understanding that action, doing, performing is the main thing in any Physical Education lesson, so we keep quiet until asked for comments, respond quickly and get on with producing action.

c Appreciating that good sporting behaviour makes such a big contribution to our enjoyment of the final part of the lesson.

Equipment: 30 bats and small balls; long rope for 'net'; 2 sets of wickets or cones; 5 canes; 10 beanbags.

Warm-up and Footwork Practices

Jogging is done with arms hanging loosely at sides and little lifting in the heels. It should be as easy as quick walking. Feel your own repeating rhythm: 'jog, 2, 3, 4; jog, 2, 3, 4.'

Skills Practices: with bat shapes and small balls

Individual practices

1 Balance ball on racket held in front of you at waist height, using wrist to control the rolling ball on the racket.

2 Gentle batting up to no more than head height, using a small wrist action, not a big elbow or shoulder hit.

3 Judge how high and far ahead to hit ball to let it bounce once before batting it up. This is a good example of 'a longer and increasingly complex sequence of movement' involving a throw, a strike and a catch.

Partner practices

Partner hitting for a catch starts off easily, aiming straight at partner. With progress, your catching partner can be made to move to one side or other, forwards or slightly back, for a variety of situations such as we experience in a game. Main coaching points are 'Hands both forwards, ready to catch. Move early to be stationary when catching. Watch ball right into hands.'

Group Practices and Small-sided Games

Tip-and-run cricket in groups of 5

Tip-and-run cricket will need a space at least as big as a third of the netball court. Any big hits must be penalised by making batter 'out' if ball goes over any of the surrounding paint lines.

Hand-tennis, 1 v 1, over low rope 'net'

In competitive hand-tennis, suggest a 5-point game, then on to a new game, possibly with a change of ends if wind, sun or slope is an advantage to either player.

Athletic activities

In shuttle relay, A to B to C to D to E to change ends. Have best of 3 races, then they all go on to practise beanbag putting as a whole group activity from a line. In 'putting', the bag is held next to your neck and pushed forwards, not taken back and thrown. In the standing high jump, the cane will be held low, at knee height by your partner. Jump from 2 feet to 2 feet.

Year 3

Lesson Plan 11 • 30-45 minutes
July

Warm-up and Footwork Practices
4—6 minutes

1 Run quietly and well, visiting every part of the playground 'classroom'. If I shut my eyes I should not be able to hear you.

2 Now add in some neat long jumps, springy high jumps and hurdling over the lines. Which is your take-off foot in long and high jumps, and which is your leading leg in hurdling?

3 Shuttle relays with class divided into teams of 4, with 2 players stationed at each side of the netball court. 'A's' race across court to touch the outstretched hand of the waiting 'B's'. The 'B's' then race to touch the waiting 'C's', while the 'A's' stay at the opposite end of the line behind the 'D's'. The race ends when your team is back in its starting place, each one having raced twice.

Group Practices in 4s: with bat shapes and small balls
8—9 minutes

Bowler bowls an easy ball to batter, who aims ball back to bowler or across to fielder. Once or twice the batter lets the ball go through to wicketkeeper to give him practice. Change around often on teacher's signal.

Group Practices and Small-sided Games
18—30 minutes

Non-stop-cricket in groups of 4
Batter must run around cone after a hit. Groups decide how to score and how to be 'out'.

Short tennis, partners, rope 'net'
You choose. Play with your partner to make a long rally or play against your partner. If the latter, decide how to start and how to score. How many points in each game? (5 is a good number.)

Tunnel-ball rounders, 4 or 5 v 4 or 5
Batting team all follow the striker to score by passing 1, 2, 3 or 4 cones before fielding team pass the ball through the tunnel of legs to end person who calls 'Stop!' Each batter has 1 strike, then teams change places.

Games

Teaching notes and NC guidance
Development over 4–5 lessons

Lesson's main emphases:

a The NC requirements to play small-sided versions of recognised games and to understand the common skills and principles in net and striking/fielding games.

b Being trusted to get on with the 3 games, sensibly and quietly, without arguments about whether or not somebody scored. Our teacher lets us decide some of our own rules. How to score, how to re-start after a score, how much space we may use, and the 1 main rule are all decisions in which we have shared.

Equipment: 8 bat shapes and small balls; 2 sets of wickets or 2 cones; 10 short-tennis rackets and 5 balls; 4 cones and 1 small ball.

Warm-up and Footwork Practices

1 After watching a group of silent runners, the observers can be asked to reflect on 'why are these runners so quiet?' The answers should include 'They are running with a good lift in the knees and the heels. They place their feet down gently. They are light and springy.'

2 The take-off or jumping foot in high and long jumps is not always the same one. They probably have not been aware of which they use for jumping or of which leads over the imaginary hurdle.

3 In the shuttle relays, ask for 'right hands to touch right hands' before outgoing runner starts to move. Race ends when last runner is standing at end of own line. Encourage a sprint-start position with legs half bent for an explosive start on being touched.

Group Practices in 4s: with bat shapes and small balls

Ask bowler to try to bowl on a 'good length' where the ball bounces about 1 metre in front of the batter for an easy hit with the bat. Encourage the 3 non-batters to stand, ready, hands both forwards towards the batter so that they are able to react quickly if the ball comes their way.

Group Practices and Small-sided Games

Non-stop cricket in groups of 4

After the batter is 'out', i.e. bowled, caught or run out, all 4 players move around clockwise, bowler to fielder to batter to wicketkeeper to bowler. Batter is also 'out' if ball leaves agreed area. This stops big hits. If unbeatable batter comes along, the teacher should ask for 'all change!' after fair share of time.

Short tennis, partners, rope 'net'

Depending on level of skill, the pairs may play co-operatively or competitively. A good way to start each rally is to drop the ball beside you to bounce up for an easy forehand stroke.

Tunnel-ball rounders, 4 or 5 v 4 or 5

In tunnel-ball rounders, the ball must be kept in the rectangle of the third of the netball court. Batting is by hand. Each cone passed gains 1 more point for the running batting team.